May Peace Be with You

May Peace Be with You

MESSAGES FROM
"THE SPOKEN WORD"

GIVEN BY
LLOYD D. NEWELL

DESERET BOOK COMPANY
SALT LAKE CITY, UTAH

Published by Deseret Book Company, P.O. Box 30178, Salt Lake City, Utah 84130.

Deseret Book is a registered trademark of Deseret Book Company.

Library of Congress Cataloging-in-Publication Data

May peace be with you : messages from "The spoken word".
   p.   cm.
   Includes bibliographical references (p.   ) and index.
   ISBN 0-87579-866-7
   1. Christian life—Mormon authors. 2. Peace of mind—Religious aspects—Mormon church. I. Music and the spoken word (Radio program)
BX8656.N49   1994
248.4'89332—dc20   94-22202
                                                    CIP

Printed in the United States of America

10 9   8   7   6   5   4   3   2   1

Contents

Contents

PART 3
The Peace of God's Gifts

Contents

PART 4
Peace and the Power of Love

PART 5
Peace with Self and Others

Contents

PART 6

The Peace of Family and Friends

Contents

Acknowledgments

THIS WEEK I RECEIVED another of a host of letters commending all who make "Music and the Spoken Word" possible. The author of the letter didn't know the names and faces of those involved, so he assigned me to communicate my thanks to them. I was honored to comply. Thanks to the other writers—James Bell, Ann Cannon, Carol Clark, Curt Dahl, Ray Haeckel, Duane Hiatt, Jayne Malan, Clifton Jolley, Truman Madsen, Dave Newbold, Neil Newell, Maurine Proctor, and Michael Robinson. Thanks to the script coordinator, the producers and technicians, Bonneville Communication's staff who produces and distributes the program worldwide, the historical figures and nameless faces who have inspired messages—and so the list gets longer. And let us not forget the conductors, organists, choir members, choir staff, and devoted listeners throughout the world. We all readily acknowledge that there would be no "spoken word" if there were not such beautiful music—and if there were not so many people the world over who thirst for inspirational broadcasting.

LLOYD D. NEWELL

PART 1

Peace in Understanding

An Understanding Heart

In the ancient Bible story, King Solomon had a dream wherein he was offered any gift he desired. He could have asked for long life, power over his enemies, or vast riches. Instead, he wanted an "understanding heart." The king knew what great leaders have learned today: an "understanding heart" opens the door to wisdom.[1]

Think for a moment if you were offered the same promise: anything you want could be yours. What comes to mind first? Of all things, why ask for an understanding heart? The wisdom of Solomon's request can teach us much about life and living.

The king seemed to know that real strength is a product of heartfelt compassion—that wisdom comes first through understanding and being empathetic toward others. After all, what can we ever really know of another's fears, frustrations, and disappointments? How can we become sensitive to others if we haven't looked into their hearts and sought for deeper understanding? Marvin J. Ashton suggests, "If we could look into each other's hearts and understand the unique challenges each of us face[s], I think we would treat each other much more gently, with more love, patience, tolerance, and care."[2] For, in our own moments of weakness, is anything more needed than an understanding heart?

Think back, perhaps to a loving parent, a dear friend, a person who seemed to understand your heart with his or her own. This heart-to-heart communication is the deepest and most meaningful. Words need not be spoken. It's conveyed through a

3

thoughtful smile, a heartfelt look, a listening ear, and a warm touch.

The eyes tell us much about our hearts. It's almost as if they're tied together by unbreakable bonds of communication. An understanding heart is communicated through loving eyes that say, "I care," "I understand," "I'm with you."

The ears communicate caring. To listen in a truly open, non-judgmental way takes courage. We may hear things we don't like; we may uncover truths we would rather not face. It's easy to thoughtlessly respond to what we hear, but it takes great patience to listen and to understand.

A touch can also speak louder than words. Many times, a hug or even a pat on the back is more penetrating than any counsel or consolation we might speak.

Therein lies the wisdom of Solomon, the powerful discovery of his choice. Of all things most desired—above all things most valued—he chose an understanding heart: a heart that could truly see, hear, and touch others.

....

1. 1 Kings 3:5–15.
2. "The Tongue Can Be a Sharp Sword," *Ensign*, May 1992, p. 20.

Having Eyes to See

THE FAMOUS AUTHOR and lecturer Helen Keller was blind and deaf from the age of two. And, late in life, when a reporter asked her what could be worse than being blind, she responded: "Having eyes to see . . . and no vision."

The lack of vision, or purposeful imagining and creating, has marked the decline of civilizations, organizations, and individuals throughout time. The Proverbs explained thousands of years ago that "where there is no vision, the people perish."[1]

If we fail to see the forest for the trees, if we lose the big picture to the consuming details before us, we concern ourselves with quick-fix solutions and never recognize deep-seated problems. We put Band-Aids on terminal wounds and replace lifelong dreams with daily demands. We engage in short-sighted planning and seldom accomplish long-term goals. We see ourselves as we are today and lose sight of whom we can become tomorrow.

But, because we are human, we can do more than just see; we can envision our future as we want it to be. We can imagine, dream, and visualize all of the great possibilities of life. All great accomplishments were first conceived in the mind. Technology is subordinate to human imagination. "We went to the moon not because of our technology but because of our imagination," said Norman Cousins. "The technology became successful only through the application not just of human intelligence but of willpower and aspiration as well."[2]

Our achievements may not be so historic. Our aspirations

may not take us to the moon. But, when we have a sense of vision, we see ourselves and others as capable, changing people—worthy of all the blessings and benefits that life has to offer. We instill a sense of "the possible" in our children. We bless other people's lives by sincerely believing and encouraging them.

Ultimately, we do all that we are capable of doing and become all that we are meant to become when we turn to God for personal vision. When we take time to ponder, to discover who we are and why we are here, we put our hands on the steering wheel of life and charge our souls with the energy of purpose.

1. Proverbs 29:18.
2. *The Celebration of Life* (New York: Harper & Row, 1974; New York: Bantam, 1991), p. 46.

The Gray Twilight

F̶AR BETTER it is to dare mighty things, to win glorious triumphs, even though checkered by failure, than to take rank with those poor spirits who neither enjoy much nor suffer much, because they live in the gray twilight that knows not victory nor defeat."[1] This wise counsel to reach beyond "the gray twilight" was penned by Theodore Roosevelt. No stranger to difficulty himself, he won and lost, dreamed and was sometimes disappointed, throughout his life. But he realized that winning and losing are not nearly as important as daring to dream.

The world's great achievements were at first—and for a time—only dreams. Someone had vision, an idea was planted, and diligent efforts were made. The seedlings of dreams produce new insights, inventions, and breakthroughs. And, once a dream takes root, it creates new dreams in its own fertile and well-worked soil, for our lives are the composite of those dreams we nurture.

What better example than windmill-slayer and country gentleman Don Quixote? In 1605, Spanish novelist Cervantes wrote his masterpiece about the idealist Quixote, a dreamer who refused to accept certain "realities" about life. You remember the story. His dreams of righting wrongs, bearing sorrow, finding beauty, and running where the brave dare not go inspire us today. Quixote's dreams were so well developed that they became his reality. Though people mocked his idealism and scathed him with the facts of life, he tenaciously held on to his dreams. And his life was all the more full.

7

Unfortunately, many of us are not willing to venture outside of "the gray twilight" and experience possible failure—or even humiliation. Those who follow their dreams know that it takes real energy and enthusiasm to reach for the stars. Perseverance in the face of overwhelming odds must fuel our efforts. But, even when life is "checkered with failure," the triumph that comes with trying, the victory that is won in the striving, will never allow us to be satisfied with mere twilight again.

1. In Art Mortell, *The Courage to Fail* (New York: McGraw-Hill, 1993), p. 194.

Failure and Resilience

WHEN ASKED what kept her going in a race no matter how much her legs hurt or her lungs burned, a high school cross country runner answered immediately: "The fear that I'll finish last."

In life, as in sports, the notion that failure may be gaining on us keeps many of us on the run. Indeed, the fear that we may stumble is a universal emotion. Who among us has not felt real anxiety at the thought of failing a class, being passed over for a promotion, ending a relationship at the other person's request?

Sometimes the grip of fear becomes so intense that it paralyzes, making it difficult for us to do all the things we need and want to do. And yet, life being what it is, we are all bound to fail at one time or another.

One young woman recalls her disastrous first and only year of teaching high school English. No matter how many hours she prepared, class did not go well. She felt stiff and wooden as she taught and knew she was fading rapidly in front of teenage students who daily grew more unruly. The only thing that kept her going was the hope that her work would eventually pay off and things would settle down. By spring, however, she had not managed to turn the experience around.

Her worst nightmare had come true. She failed at something she had wanted to do. She was a failure even though she had tried hard.

The months that followed her decision to find another line of work were filled with difficult, bitter emotions. Yet, during that

9

period, the young woman discovered she was far more resilient than she'd ever dreamed. While things were rough sometimes, she was learning a lot of good things about herself and that she was just fine. Now, looking back, the young woman says the great lesson she learned is not that we should avoid failure at all costs, but that we can survive failure.

There is an inherent resilience deeply rooted in each of our spirits that can help us make a comeback—a slow, painful one, perhaps not always of our own choosing—but a comeback still the same. Indeed, resilience is the special gift of all living things—the force that makes plants seek the sun after a damaging storm. It is as though the psalmist's words are written on our souls: "Weeping may endure for a night, but joy cometh in the morning."[1]

1. Psalm 30:5.

This Will I Do

THE CITIZENS OF ATHENS gathered to choose which of two architects would erect a great building. The first, in a long discourse, boasted of how magnificent his work would be—how detailed, how strong, how monumental. By the time he finished, he had all but convinced the crowd. Then, his competitor rose to speak. "O, Athenians," he told them, "what this man says, I will do."[1]

He reminded the Athenians how easily promises pass the lips and how rare it is to find individuals who follow through on the pledges they make. We all know people like this; they brag about the great things they're going to do when the time is right or when the breaks come their way. And so, they bide their time waiting for life to begin, and all the while it keeps passing them by.

The Roman poet Horace wrote that he who deferred the hour of living well "is like the fool who keeps waiting for the river to run by so he can cross. But the river still runs on, and will run on, with constant course, to ages without end."[2]

So it is with time. And they who wait for the right moment to begin life will lament with the poet who wrote, "I have spent my life stringing and unstringing my instrument and all the while the song I had meant to sing has been left unsung."[3]

It is not enough to wish for what we want; we must work to achieve our dreams. Leonardo da Vinci claimed, "God sells us all things at the price of labor."[4]

Work is the miracle which transforms vision into reality. It

11

"is the grand cure of all the maladies and miseries that ever beset mankind."[5] "It banishes boredom, vice and poverty."[6]

Whatever your worthwhile dreams, begin them. We can't afford to be numbered among those who spend their precious energy boasting of what they will do in the future or explaining why they haven't done what they promised in the past.

Time is too precious, too short, to waste on broken promises. The Athenian builder knew what we must all come to know: it is not enough to intend to do things. We must do them.

1. Montaigne, *Essays I.25,* translated by Charles Cotton in *Great Books of the Western World,* edited by Robert Maynard Hutchins (Chicago: Encyclopaedia Britannica, 1982), p. 76.
2. *Epistles I.2, 40.*
3. Rabindranath Tagore.
4. Richard L. Evans, *Richard Evans' Quote Book* (Salt Lake City: Publisher's Press, 1971), p. 44.
5. Thomas Carlyle, Rectorial address at Edinburgh, 2 April 1886.
6. Voltaire, *Candide,* translated by Robert M. Adams (New York: W. W. Norton, 1991), p. 74.

Doers of the Word

THE APOSTLE JAMES gave this wise counsel on Christian conduct: "But be ye doers of the word, and not hearers only, deceiving your own selves."[1] That is good counsel in all areas of human endeavor. From neighborhoods to nations, nothing happens without doers. And, as James said, we deceive ourselves when we substitute anything else for doing.

A business consultant once noted that spinners of a new idea are a dime a dozen, but they don't always help a company succeed. In fact, people who go up and down the halls tossing off ideas with reckless abandon can be more disruptive than useful to an organization. "But," he said, "give me a person who can put new and better ways into practice, and I'll pay his weight in gold."

These priceless people who put plans into practice are the doers of the word. They put bolts and rivets into dreams and aspirations. The doers may be reading to children, writing books, building bridges, plowing fields, teaching students, or assisting the elderly or disabled. Whatever their chosen work, they are busily about it.

Good planning is important. But let us not confuse planning with performing, wishing with working. Even a mediocre plan carried out with enthusiasm will accomplish more than a grand design that never gets off the drawing board.

We have seen the shakeup and collapse of many carefully planned governments and economies. On paper, their designs may have looked feasible. But, in the actual daily running of their countries, there are far too few doers and too little incentive to produce.

The warning is clear to all of us. No matter how abundantly we may be blessed, we must continually be about the business of doing good work. It has been said that a society that glorifies philosophy and denigrates plumbing will soon find itself in trouble. Neither its philosophies nor its pipes will hold water. In fact, the most effective philosophies are those that inspire good actions among their followers. History is lettered with the wreckage of utopias that crumpled under the weight of belief without action.

As with nations and society, so it is in our individual lives. All about us are people who need help, problems that need solutions, work waiting to be accomplished. For the good of others and ourselves, we need to be doing. The secret to success and satisfaction in life lies in work well done.

A wise religious leader was known to have prominently displayed on his desk two simple words written on a small plaque: DO IT! In other words, don't just wish—DO; don't just pray for people—DO for people!

Let us remember that intending is not doing. Considering is not doing. Even assigning and delegating is not doing. Only doing is doing. And only doing changes and improves the world. Only doing changes and improves the doer.

Planning, organizing, and preparing may be the blossoms, but doing brings fruit. And, as Jesus said, "By their fruits ye shall know them."[2]

1. James 1:22.
2. Matthew 7:20.

Do Your Best

Do your best, be good, work hard." Each morning, those words cheerfully rang out from a young mother as she sent her children to school. And, year after year, those same words of encouragement continued. That motto of sorts has now passed to a second generation as her children send their children to school with the same refrain.

"Do your best, be good, work hard." This common-sense slogan echoes, in slightly different words, from the pages of *The Agony and the Ecstasy*, Irving Stone's classic novel about sculptor and artist Michelangelo. The talented, young Michelangelo sought advice from his spiritual leader one day and received this counsel: "Do the best that is in you, or nothing at all. There is only a God-given numbers of years in which to work and fulfill yourself. Don't squander them." When he died many decades later, Michelangelo had, indeed, become one of the most prolific artists of all time. And it was Michelangelo's contemporary, Leonardo da Vinci, who cried out: "O Lord, thou givest us everything at the price of an effort."[1]

No matter what our level of talent, education, or experience, we can still "do our best"—within the realm of our capability. In so doing, we need only be concerned with getting ahead of ourselves, not others. Perhaps the Lord also would counsel: "Do your best, be good, work hard."

At times, however, we fail. But, as long as our effort was honest, diligent, and to the best of our ability, it cannot be considered

15

a failure. After all, as the old saying goes, the way to succeed is to double your failure rate. For instance, in the same year Babe Ruth set a major league baseball record for home runs, he also set a record for strike-outs.

Of course, that young mother's admonition to "be good" is no less important than her call to "do your best" and "work hard." For, undoubtedly, God is interested—first and foremost—in how well we obey His commandments. As author Victor Hugo once suggested, "Good actions are the invisible hinges on the doors of heaven."[2]

One of Christianity's beloved hymns asks, "Have I done any good in the world today? Have I helped anyone in need? Have I cheered up the sad and made someone feel glad? If not, I have failed indeed."[3]

As we begin each day, let us then pause and consider the words of encouragement offered by a wise, young mother to "do your best, be good, and work hard."

1. In Charles L. Wallis, ed., *The Treasure Chest* (New York: Harper & Row, 1965), p. 81.
2. Ibid., p. 112.
3. "Have I Done Any Good?" in *Hymns of The Church of Jesus Christ of Latter-day Saints* (Salt Lake City: The Church of Jesus Christ of Latter-day Saints, 1985), no. 223.

The Blessing of the Boll Weevil

SOME YEARS AGO, boll weevils infested the cotton crops in Enterprise, Alabama. For two consecutive years, the boll weevils plagued the cotton plants and threatened the farmers' livelihood until, finally, they decided to grow peanuts in place of cotton. Today, a statue honoring the boll weevil occupies a prominent place in the small town of Enterprise. It serves as a visual reminder of what came to be a blessing in disguise. The boll weevil, considered at first a curse, was the catalyst for a more lucrative source of income. Peanuts have proven to be a much more profitable commodity for the appropriately named town of Enterprise. Those farmers realized that the best way to fight against the boll weevil was to actively seek out other opportunities.[1]

Often, the heat of adversity forces us to pursue unchartered courses and take unexpected turns. But those very problems may inspire us to find solutions that, ultimately, lead to more abundant living. The comforting wisdom of Cervantes teaches us that, when one door shuts, another always opens.

Certainly, it can be difficult to wait for that "other" door to open when one has just been slammed in our face—or if one is slowly closing in front of us. But perhaps the closing of that door is in itself an opening—an occasion to learn patience and adopt the refining attitude of faith. From the perspective of years, we often look back with a sigh of relief. Not getting a particular job that, at the time, we so desperately wanted left us available to receive a better opportunity later. A rejection in our professional or even personal pursuits may have led to the opening for which we are now so grateful. The alternate path that emerged from adverse circumstances may be the one that makes all the difference in our lives.

With our limited perspective, it may be hard to believe in other possibilities when present disappointments can be so over-shadowing. But those difficulties may be just what are needed to make a breakthrough, develop a new friendship, and create a greater opportunity to contribute. Our talents may be best developed when we go in a direction other than the one we had planned on. We may make a difference in our own life—and in someone else's—when we are forced to face a challenging and unexpected alternative.

Just ask the folks in Enterprise, Alabama. The once-cursed boll weevil is now celebrated as a blessing.

1. Fred Pryor, *The Energetic Manager* (Englewood Cliffs, New Jersey: Prentice Hall, 1987), p. 43.

The Law of the Harvest

THE LAW OF THE HARVEST is an age-old formula for success: "Whatsoever a man soweth, that shall he also reap."[1] Today, we hear it in expressions like "you are what you eat," "you'll pick what you plant," and "your return is only as great as your investment." Though the metaphors may change, the message remains the same: we receive according to how we have given or how diligently we have worked. Whether our investment be of time, talents, means, or even of self, the reward is always proportionate.

Those who have found success—in one of its many forms—are those who have worked to achieve it. The great inventor Thomas Edison openly admitted: "I never did anything worth doing by accident, nor did any of my inventions come by accident. They came by work."[2] With a similar orientation toward his life's work, the renowned poet William Wordsworth wrote his greatest poem about his *labor* to become a poet. In *The Prelude,* he describes the "fair seed-time" of his soul when, as a boy in England, he learned from nature—even while at play.[3]

No matter how great our efforts, the harvest is never just a product of our own labors. The seeds we sow and the plants we nourish grow only when the heavens pour rain upon them and when the sun showers them with its life-giving rays. In other words, our harvest is never entirely our own. All of our efforts and all of our means are not just enhanced by the Lord's blessings, but ultimately they are His. For, as Isaiah has written: "We are all the work of thy hands."[4] And those laborers who recognize the Lord's handiwork in their lives will always reap more plentifully.

But, even while we rely on the Lord for an abundant harvest, we must faithfully plow and water the fields. Paul taught the Corinthians: "He that planteth and he that watereth are one: and every man shall receive his own reward according to his own labour. For we are labourers together with God."[5] The Lord has given us minds and bodies for a purpose. We are to use them. And in no greater way do we abuse these God-given resources than when we fail to develop them—fail to put them to work. Let us plant well and cultivate anew, that we might reap the bounteous harvest that God intended for us all.

1. Galatians 6:7.
2. In Richard L. Evans, *Richard Evans' Quote Book* (Salt Lake City: Publishers Press, 1971), p. 48.
3. Book 1, line 290.
4. Isaiah 64:8.
5. 1 Corinthians 3:8, 9.

The Importance of Moral Virtues

NEARLY TWO THOUSAND YEARS AGO, Marcus Aurelius Antoninus made a statement that still rings true—one that may have greater application today than it did in Roman days.

He said, "Never value anything as profitable to thyself which shall compel thee to break thy promise, [or] to lose thy self-respect."[1]

He was aware that our word is one of the most precious things we own. Once it is given, we must do everything within our power not to break it, for a string of broken promises will soon limit the effectiveness of our actions.

Even more important, the insightful comment relates to moral guidance—an area where many observers believe our society has lost its bearing.

Teaching right from wrong was once as basic a task in education as teaching the three R's, but moral guidance has all but disappeared from the curriculum. Perhaps there has been a fear of alienating parents or interfering with a student's personal beliefs; but there is a crying need for basic rules of the road on such timeless principles as the value of honesty and integrity, of courage and compassion, of keeping one's word.

In fact, we might all benefit from examining our feelings about what is right and what is wrong.

As one noted American educator puts it, moral life is not a matter of ordeals or dilemmas but a conscious decision for decency. And parents can teach those basic virtues most effectively by the way they live. They are proven virtues that make society work and make life worth living.

As Marcus Aurelius pointed out, never losing our self-respect—being true to ourselves—also brings happiness and personal joy, the inner harmony and feeling that our lives are focused. That's something all of our souls yearn for.

Thomas Jefferson also wrote about moral virtues. When he referred to happiness, he wasn't thinking of mere pleasure-getting or status-seeking. He wrote in terms of the traditional philosophical conception of happiness—that happiness is "a life well lived or a good life as a whole."

Surely more of us have learned that pursuit of happiness in not "doing our own thing" but doing the right thing. True happiness depends upon living by our inner sense of right and wrong. It means possessing moral virtues that are within our power to acquire. If we don't acquire them, we have no one to blame but ourselves.

That's the key to a happy or good life, and it is essentially the same for all human beings. It depends upon the practice of moral virtues—of never doing anything that makes us break our word or lose our self-respect. We gain strength from many sources, not the least of which is strength from within—the strength to achieve victory over ourselves.

1. *Meditations*, translated by George Long (Indiana: Gateway Editions, 1956), p. 25.

The Things That Matter

SOMETIMES WE MEASURE our self-worth by our net worth. We may get so caught up in acquiring and possessing that our identity is defined by our income. We may compare the home we own, the clothes we wear, and the car we drive to other homes, clothes, and cars—one day feeling superior because of what we *have* and the next day feeling inferior because of what we *don't have*. We can never get enough of what we don't need. All the "things" in the world will never bring us lasting peace and real joy.

But we are worth more than all of our possessions—no matter how wealthy or how poor we may be. There is more than materialism to make life worth living. If we build our lives only on the "things" of this world, when those "things" break down and wear out, so will we. But, when we build on eternal truths, lasting relationships, and the "things" that really matter, we will abide the letdowns of life.

The words of a "lowly" Galilean, offered some two thousand years ago, put acquisitiveness into perspective: "For what is a man profited, if he shall gain the whole world, and lose his own soul?"[1] How can we put a price tag on honesty, character, and integrity? How can we assess the monetary value of family relationships, trusted companionships, and Godly kinship? What is the price of health and happiness? What "thing" can replace trust and love?

The gifted scientist and philosopher Albert Einstein said: "It is a mistake often made in this country to measure things by the amount of money they cost."[2] Unless we have given our minds and hearts to spiritual insights, deep understandings, the "things" that really matter, we may be off balance—trying to measure the meaningful with the material.

An unknown writer wisely observed that a person wrapped up in himself makes a very small package. And we could also say: a person wrapped up in all the possessions money can buy is equally small—if the "things" of everlasting importance are not part of the package.

When we come to be genuinely concerned with pleasing God more than pleasing anyone else—even ourselves—then our need to acquire and possess will decrease, our joy will increase, and His blessings can surround us.

1. Matthew 16:26.

2. *Einstein: A Portrait* (Corte Madera, California: Pomegranate Artbooks, 1984), p. 70. (All quotations © Hebrew University of Jerusalem.)

Patterns of Constancy

Nature has a steady, sure rhythm about it that we are reminded of in this autumn season. In lakes and ponds across the land, the ducks have come again—visitors on their way south. As they did last year and the year before, their early morning sounds tell us it is fall. A change is coming to the land. Soon the air will have a chill to it, the days will be short, and the leaves will become vibrant with color. It's just this way every year.

Here is a pattern of constancy that tells us one season is becoming another.

As on earth, so is it in the heavens. We find these marvelous patterns of constancy. The sky is a place of order. The North Star, Polaris, is an ancient symbol of Jesus Christ. Through the night, it is unmoving, while the other stars seem to dance in great circles around it. Gaze into the nighttime sky, and we are reassured that nature has a steady rhythm about it.

Surely all this steadiness and constancy in earth and in heaven is a reflection of the Lord who created it. We who always yearn to know something more about His personality find Him when we look at His creations. He is sure, unchanging, working in patterns of constancy because He is constant.

"For do we not read that God is the same yesterday, today, and forever, and in him there is no variableness, neither shadow of changing?"[1]

What a contrast this is to the world in which we live, where so little is constant. Governments come and go. The leader who promises one thing may go on to do another. Economies are unstable, and popular opinion is fickle. What appears to offer us security today may disintegrate before our eyes tomorrow.

We live in an age of stress, where much of the insecurity of the world has filtered into our personal lives. Often, we cannot enjoy this moment, for the anxieties of the next are always pulling us on. Our nerves, too often, are rattled—our hearts uneasy.

Many will give us solutions for these problems, but often they are false solutions. The only solution for the stress and insecurity of this world is to reconnect with the author of peace and constancy.

As the Lord said, "Peace I leave with you, my peace I give unto you: not as the world giveth, give I unto you. Let not your heart be troubled, neither let it be afraid."[2]

The Lord built His patterns of constancy into this earth to assure us that He is there and He is unchanging. When the world rattles around us, we can turn to Him and be renewed. We can, as Robert Frost wrote, "choose something like a star to stay our minds on and be staid."[3]

1. Mormon 9:9.
2. John 14:27.
3. "Choose Something Like a Star," *Steeple Bush* (New York: Henry Holt and Company, 1947).

The Seasons of Life

NOTHING IS SO CONSTANT as change. And nothing is as change-able as life. Each day brings with it different circumstances, unexpected opportunities, and new challenges. Just as sure as children grow up and have children of their own, life breeds change—and with it, growth. The cycle of children becoming parents and parents becoming grandparents teaches this great lesson: "To every thing there is a season, and a time to every purpose under the heaven."[1]

Whether we *have* children or not, this principle of parenting—of adjusting to the seasons of life—tells us about the nature of our existence. And it reminds us that, because change and growth are essential parts of life's package, new skills, new perspectives, even renewed patience are essential. As long as we are living and breathing, changing circumstances give us opportunities for growth.

At work, don't we usually change jobs or get more responsibility just when we are feeling comfortable with the old? In school, didn't it usually happen that new material was presented just when we were understanding yesterday's assignments? And even on the playground, wasn't there always one more game to learn just about the time we had mastered the last? As is the case with every stage of life, parenting demands ongoing development. About the time we become accustomed to rearing children, those children become adults and require a different—and maybe even more challenging—stewardship.

Peace in Understanding

The seasons of life that take us from child to parent to grandparent tell us much about our reasons for being. We *are* that we might learn, grow, and change. And, because each of us is involved in cycles of growth, our journey is one of adapting to life's latest season. While we plant seeds in our own way and harvest blessings on different timetables, as human beings we are ever planting, growing, and blossoming.

....

1. Ecclesiastes 3:1.

"Death Shall Be No More"

AMONG THE CERTAINTIES of life is death. Sometimes during our sojourn, it knocks at the door of a loved one. And we who are left to walk through empty rooms and sit in quiet corners experience the pain of loss. The bittersweet reminders are everywhere. We look at familiar photos, pause over personal belongings, and hold on to the memories preserved in journals and other writings. We become acquainted with grief and familiar with heartache.

But we need not despair. For our own sake, we must not. We can find solace in the midst of sorrow and peace in spite of the pain. Today, as we remember those who have passed on, let us find comfort in the words of Paul: "O death, where is thy sting? O grave, where is thy victory?"[1]

The grave's only victory is in our refusal to be comforted. As long as we concentrate on our loss, death overshadows life—both our own and our departed loved ones'. But, by realizing that life does go on, death loses its sting and our wounds begin to heal. The poet John Donne waged his own battle of belief. "Death, thou shalt die," he proclaimed. And, in so doing, he reaffirmed the reality of everlasting life:

> One short sleep past, we wake eternally
> and death shall be no more; Death, thou shalt die.[2]

The realization that life is eternal and that "death shall be no more" seems the natural understanding of a child. Not long after a little girl's teenage sister died, this hopeful child asked her parents

29

why everyone was so sad. "She's just living in heaven now," the five-year-old explained. "We don't need to cry anymore." When rooms become painfully empty and quiet, when words fail to express the sorrow we feel, we can remember the wisdom of a child.

Even when death touches the most tender places of our hearts, we can let God's peace in. By replacing fear with faith and exchanging grief for gratitude, we can come to terms with this painful but temporary loss, for He who blessed us with life here also promises life hereafter.

1. 1 Corinthians 15:55.

2. "Death, Be Not Proud," in M. H. Abrams, ed., *The Norton Anthology of English Literature,* 5th ed. (New York: W. W. Norton & Company, 1986), p. 1099.

In Memory of One Who Sleeps

TODAY, A HUSHED NOTE, a hymn for those who sleep, for those whom memory keeps alive. For, surely, there is none among us who does not carry the sweet but painful reminiscence of someone who has faded into the darkness and the silence—perhaps a father, mother, daughter, son, a husband or wife—someone we laughed with, cried with, lived for, and now mourn for.

"Parting is such sweet sorrow,"[1] wrote the poet: sorrowful because we miss those whom we love and sweet because we love those whom we mourn.

Yes, we could easily eliminate the sorrow of death by simply erasing love from life—blotting out all hint of fondness, every taste of affection, each clue of devotion. Gone would be the holding of hands between loved ones who have faced life's trials together, gone the timid gaze of first love beneath the shrouded lamppost, gone the goodnight beam of pride above the cradle, gone the photographs of war heroes upon the mantel—all gone, traded for fear of pain, for dread of temporary death.

But who would barter love for apathy? Who would give up the sacred memories of life to avoid the pang of death? Hopefully, no one.

Our true condolence and pity, then, are not only offered to those who mourn, but also to those who have had no cause to mourn: not only to the mother who longs to be with her dead baby, but to her also who has held no child; not only to the widow or widower who aches for the companionship of a departed sweet-

31

heart, but also to those who have no sweetheart to miss; not only to the son or daughter who grieves for loving parents, but also for those children who have longed for a loving home.

Mourning is a form of rejoicing—a gratitude for love, for memories, for life.

Today, then, we sing to comfort, to share the understanding that mourning is the fair price we pay for the dividends of love.

And remember that even mourning is a temporary grief—for death itself is as short-lived as life. Just as night's darkness is swallowed by morning light, soon the sting of earthly partings will be healed in the joy of future reunions, where we can love forever.

---

1. William Shakespeare, *Romeo and Juliet,* act II, scene 2, line 185.

PART 2

Peace through Faith and Hope

The Power of Hope

....

ONE THING we all have in common is that we make mistakes. We all experience setbacks and sorrows. But, just as nothing is more universal than human fallibility and disappointment, there is nothing more essential than hope. In the words of Samuel Johnson, "It is necessary to hope, . . . for hope itself is happiness."[1]

Situations that are hostile to the human spirit spring up all around us. Such unfavorable conditions would have us believe that defeat is inevitable—that there is no tomorrow. The powers of negativism would have us mock hope and destroy faith.

But, at such moments, we must separate ourselves from our shortcomings and our setbacks. And remember that failure is an event; it is never a person. Our life may be disrupted by disappointments and shattered by sorrows, but hope in today and faith in tomorrow are what give purpose and meaning to life. Our bodies, minds, and spirits may not be as strong as we'd like, but we always have room to grow, to experience, to change, and to hope.

The world in which we live is a model of hope. Out of the hardened, winter earth come forth soft, spring tulips. Out of the den of hibernation comes the revitalized bear. From within the protective chrysalis emerges the delicate butterfly. Year after year, such natural happenings remind us of the fresh start, the new life, the hope that the Lord promises to each of us. "For in him we live, and move, and have our being."[2]

As children of God, we are neither hopeless nor helpless. Because of His love and forgiveness, we are much more potential

35

than we are actuality. In our efforts to improve, we may get discouraged and dispirited; but we, with the psalmist, can say, "In thee, O Lord, do I hope."[3]

We may suffer setbacks, endure sorrows, and experience more than we think is our fair share of disappointment. We may struggle to understand many things about this life. But we can trust in the promise of a better life: in being reunited with departed loved ones, in having our ailments healed, our grievances redressed, and feeling the warmth of God's love.

It takes great courage to be imperfect and yet hopeful. It takes real faith to live with hope amid despair. But, when we have faith in the Lord, we have power in the present and hope in the future. And that hope will help give us "peace in this life, and eternal life in the world to come."[4] Let us sing, with hope, the words of the song:

> O God, touch Thou my aching heart,
> And calm my troubled, haunting fears.
> Let hope and faith, transcendent, pure,
> Give strength and peace beyond my tears.[5]

1. In Richard L. Evans, *Richard Evans' Quote Book* (Salt Lake City: Publishers Press, 1971), p. 146.
2. Acts 17:28.
3. Psalm 38:15.
4. Doctrine and Covenants 59:23.
5. Gordon B. Hinckley, "The Empty Tomb Bore Testimony," *Ensign*, May 1988, p. 66.

Hold Fast with Faith

In this season of new beginnings, in these times of uncertainty, we must hold fast with faith to the everlasting things. As Robert Louis Stevenson has so timelessly written, "Whether on the first of January or on the thirty-first of December, faith is a good word to end on."[1]

All worthy ventures begin and end with faith, for faith is essential to living. The entrepreneur who, with positive belief, creates a new product or service exercises faith. The parent who believes in the greatness of a child plants seeds of faith. And the person who, day after day, quietly and courageously faces adversity exercises faith just by living with hope.

Often, the most profound demonstrations of faith go unnoticed, unacclaimed. We may not receive the thunderous applause of the world. In fact, we may have to applaud for ourselves as we faithfully make efforts to improve and change, for it takes great faith to believe in yourself when others don't. And it takes great courage to exercise faith when some would have us believe that faith is folly and belief is foolish.

We constantly need the strength, power, and peace that come from faith in God. Such faith can help us to have hope in the present and belief in our future. As we daily struggle to be more patient, more loving, more trusting—and more trustworthy—faith can be a "spiritual lifeboat" that keeps us afloat when we feel like we're drowning. When the turbulent water surrounds, even when the dam breaks, faith gives us the assurance that "this too shall pass" and that a day will soon come when sorrow will cease, pain will end, and joy will fill our hearts. During the worst moments, perhaps the best we can do is hold on with faith until the storm subsides. Looking to our Maker helps us keep our heads above water in these most trying times.

For real faith is more than just positive thoughts and hopeful words. As the Lord Himself has commanded, "Have faith in God."[2] And, "What things soever ye desire, when ye pray, believe that ye receive them, and ye shall have them."[3] So, faith is an active belief in God, demanding humility and patience. It is the result of much praying, working, and enduring.

A glorious peace can fill our hearts as we hold fast with faith and realize that "whether on the first of January or on the thirty-first of December, faith is a good word to end on."

1. In Hugh B. Brown, *Vision and Valor* (Salt Lake City: Bookcraft, 1971), p. 71.
2. Mark 11:22.
3. Mark 11:24.

We Walk by Faith

THE PROCESS OF SPIRITUAL GROWTH can be long and hard. Our natural tendency is to resist change, take the course of least resistance, and focus on the mundane matters of this world. But, when we exercise faith in God, we have hope in the future and power in the present.

Spiritual growth takes place when we first desire to change—and then begin to exercise even a particle of faith. There is no more powerful force on this earth than the spiritual strength that comes through faith in our Heavenly Father. Faith is the essence of the Lord's message: faith in God, faith in other people, faith in ourselves, and faith in life itself.

Christ taught, "If ye have faith . . . nothing shall be impossible unto you,"[1] and "All things are possible to him that believeth."[2] When we really believe in God and exercise faith in His power and love, our belief becomes faith and our faith becomes trust.

Of course, there is much we cannot understand—not now. But faith carries us through the things we don't comprehend: the pain, hurt, sorrow, and disappointments of this world. There will ever be doubts and fears in tomorrow. But, for today, we can be comforted that He knows us—and He loves us.

Who knows all the answers? He who knows everything about us and about this world. He who wants us to have everlasting joy. And all He expects from us is a teachable spirit, a contrite heart, and a willingness to keep His commandments—to seek for Him with faith.

Because "faith is the substance of things hoped for, the evidence of things not seen,"[3] it takes real courage to believe. We have to trust Him for so much and rely on Him for so many things. Just as the night follows day, we can have confidence that He is there for us.

Victor Hugo gave this advice: "Have courage for the great sorrows of life, and patience for the small ones; and when you have laboriously accomplished your daily task, go to sleep in peace. God is awake."[4]

No matter how tired we may be and how weary our efforts become, God *is* awake and watching over each of us. When we humble ourselves to know that we owe Him our lives, our souls, the very air we breathe, we begin to walk the road of faith—with God.

1. Matthew 17:20.
2. Mark 9:23.
3. Hebrews 11:1.
4. In Richard L. Evans, *Richard Evans' Quote Book* (Utah: Publisher's Press, 1971), p. 139.

Because There Is a God

THE RUSSIAN NOVELIST Leo Tolstoy spent five long years writing his masterwork, *War and Peace*. Toward the end of this epic novel, the central character, Pierre, discovers faith—and, with it, a new attitude toward life. The novelist writes of Pierre's struggle with "that dreadful question, 'What for?'" He tells of the moment when, at last, Pierre's doubts "no longer existed for him. To that question, 'What for,' a simple answer was now always ready in his soul: 'Because there is a God.'"[1]

What for? What is the purpose of life? The great quest to find meaning is a pressing concern for many. We search and study, ponder and pray, hoping to acquire that precious perspective of simple faith. The truth is, all of us have unanswered questions. Only He who knows everything about life—and about us—knows all the answers.

God is mindful of each of His children. We need only be patient and humbly fortify our faith that He might make His purposes manifest in our lives. Pierre searched for answers all his life, looking for "that great inscrutable infinite *something*." Until finally, "he learned . . . by direct feeling . . . that God is here and everywhere." Without even realizing it, Pierre had been looking for faith all along: "not faith in any kind of rule, or words, or ideals, but faith in an ever-living, ever-manifest God."[2]

He learned that, because there is a God, none of us is ever really alone. God is the ever-present source of truth, light, and love. While the philosophies of men and women change almost with the seasons, the Lord and His teachings never change. He is "the same yesterday, to day, and for ever."[3] Even though "from everlasting to everlasting [He is] the same unchangeable God,"[4] He desires that we change, grow, and learn.

Because "the course of the Lord is one eternal round,"[5] He knows us without beginning or end. With our limited outlook, we may lose sight of our eternal possibilities. But God sees beyond the here and now. He knows that life's lessons can refine and define us. With His perfect and personal love, He encourages us to understand our inherent worth and to discover the greater purposes of life.

From start to finish, we experience growing pains. We struggle to find meaning and identity. But we can be sustained by the sweet whisperings of our soul that recall the divinity within us. That is the great process of life and living. With a teachable spirit and a faith-filled heart, the "what for's" can be answered by the sublime and heartfelt understanding of a believer: "Because there is a God."

1. *War and Peace,* translated by Louise and Aylmer Maude, in *Great Books of the Western World* (Chicago: Encyclopaedia Britannica, 1990), p. 631.
2. Ibid.
3. Hebrews 13:8.
4. Doctrine and Covenants 20:17.
5. 1 Nephi 10:19.

The Gracious Hand
Which Preserves Us

During the darkest period of United States' history, the president proclaimed a National Fast Day to ask Providence for peace and to remind citizens from whence came their strength. "We have been the recipients of the choicest bounties of Heaven," said Abraham Lincoln. "We have grown in numbers, wealth, and power.... But we have forgotten God. We have forgotten the gracious hand which preserved us . . . and multiplied and enriched and strengthened us; and we have vainly imagined, in the deceitfulness of our hearts, that all these blessings were produced by some superior wisdom and virtue of our own. . . . We have become too self-sufficient . . . , too proud to pray to the God that made us."[1]

Indeed, President Lincoln knew the country needed divine guidance, both in times of prosperity and during civil war. Regardless of the historical context, this message of divine dependence is timeless, even as it is timely. The nature of the battles may or may not change. We could be involved in moral struggles, social standoffs, or physical warfare. But the cry for divinity is just as necessary.

Our knees must bend not only in the heat of battle but also in the warmth of prosperity. When all seems well, we so easily forget the Author of Peace, let alone the causes for which we—and others—have fought. Perhaps we lose sight of principles that once saved us, the values and devotions that are our lifeblood. If we let peace turn into self-serving complacency, we live with a false sense of confidence, thinking that, while everything is under control, we have only ourselves to thank for it—and, conversely, only ourselves to turn to when all is not so well.

Even now, we may find ourselves struggling to survive on one of life's front lines. We may ache inside with the pains of a broken heart, or maybe we battle with an aging or breaking body. Now, as before, there is One who knows every soul—and nation—in anguish. Have we forgotten Him?

As the president and as a person, Abraham Lincoln knew both war and peace. And, like each of us, after the applause died down and friends and foes departed, he was alone with God. This president spent a lot of time on his knees: seeking wisdom and guidance, supplicating the Almighty for direction, thanking Him for blessings. He did not forget from whence came his strength.

And history has not forgotten him. Many years after the Civil War, Katherine Lee Bates wrote inspired words of praise, a lyrical reminder of the America for which Lincoln lived and died—an America made beautiful by the Creator of us all:

> Oh, beautiful for spacious skies,
> For amber waves of grain,
> For purple mountain majesties
> Above the fruited plain.
> America! America! God shed His grace
> on thee.[2]

---

1. In Suzy Platt, ed., *Respectfully Quoted: A Dictionary of Quotations Requested from the Congressional Research Service* (Washington: Library of Congress, 1989), p. 12.

2. "America the Beautiful," *Hymns of The Church of Jesus Christ of Latter-day Saints* (Salt Lake City: The Church of Jesus Christ of Latter-day Saints, 1985), no. 338.

Wait on the Lord

THE ONSET OF SPRING appears to be an overnight sensation. Almost before our eyes, the world is splashed with spring's vibrant colors. The ground that just yesterday seemed hard and cold now gives way to blossoming flowers: a crocus appears; a daffodil opens; a tulip pushes the remains of winter away. And all of this seems to happen in just a day or two. But what we don't notice is the season of growth that took place beneath the earth, the microscopic milestones worked toward the whole winter through.

And so it goes with many of the achievements and attributes we desire most. In admiring—even in striving for—the rites of spring, we sometimes forget the difficult but essential passage of winter. We may want something, and want it now, not stopping to consider its price or value. And, if it is given to us without the preparation of earning it, we may find that we really don't want or appreciate it after all. In the same regard, if we don't receive a blessing after doing what we thought necessary to earn it, if the Lord's timetable doesn't comply with our own, we may likewise lose spring's colorful blossoms to winter's lingering blues.

The psalmist wrote, "Wait on the Lord: be of good courage, and he shall strengthen thine heart."[1] During the winters of our life, we may wonder why and for how long we must face certain hardships. But, as we look to the Lord for strength and patiently wait for spring, the very trials we long to uproot will give way to blossoms of faith. "Little by little, through patience and longsuffering, thou shalt conquer by the help of God," wrote Thomas à Kempis.[2]

Even though our progress may be invisible to the eye, little by little, the season of turmoil will pass and—as if overnight—peace will fill our hearts.

Of our own devices, perhaps we would shorten one season and lengthen another. Without knowing the beginning from the end, we might want to assign our own beginnings and endings to the experiences that the Lord, in His wisdom, has given us—and, in the process, deny ourselves of the attendant virtues that grow out of rainy seasons.

The resurrected Lord reassured His grieving apostles, and each of us in turn, "I am with you alway[s], even unto the end of the world."[3] On the darkest of winter days, when the sight of a spring blossom seems worlds away, the Light of the World would shower us with His perfect and redeeming love.

1. Psalm 27:14.
2. In Richard L. Evans, *Richard Evans' Quote Book* (Salt Lake City: Publisher's Press, 1971), p. 156.
3. Matthew 28:20.

He Will Be with Us

Many ask why they have so much adversity in their lives. Why doesn't the Lord help them? Why doesn't He answer their prayers? The life of the believer is not easy, even though many blessings may come because of a desire to follow the teachings of Christ.

We cannot assume that the more righteous a person is or the more diligently he or she keeps the Lord's commandments, the less he or she will suffer. The Lord does not always answer our prayers the way we want Him to. And He doesn't always spare us from adversity. His promise is that we will be blessed, even though our blessing may simply be the strength to endure suffering and adversity.

We will find that the Lord gives us comfort when we seek help. He gives us strength to bear the burden, and, thus, He is still able to accomplish His purposes. But the relief usually comes quietly and naturally, so that, unless we are in tune and develop a sensitivity to the way in which the Lord works, we may not recognize that relief occurred.

Some people grow bitter when they watch a loved one suffer. Some would charge God with unkindness, with indifference, and with injustice. But we know so little. And our judgment is so limited. We judge the Lord's way from our own narrow view. In time, we will understand. We will find the answers we seek. But, for the present, we must make sure we are living Christlike lives—keeping the commandments, being our brother's keeper, and showing a measure of love to those around us. And that may simply have to be enough to help us through the difficult times.

As we ponder our lives, we usually find that, as one trial comes to a close, another takes its place. We are rarely entirely free of adversity. Each of us has his or her own personal bag of rocks that we're carrying around. Each one is different. Your neighbor's load may not look heavy to you. And yours may not look heavy to your neighbor. But we're all in this together—each carries the load that gives the particular individual the most opportunity for growth.

Ironically, one of the easiest ways to lighten our load is to reach down and help carry someone else's. There is no greater cure for our own wounds than to dress the wounds of someone else.

We must remember, too, that, when life is always easy, there is no trial of faith. As medical research has shown, bones grow strongest along lines of stress. It was a saying of Milton that "who best can suffer, best can do." The work of many of the greatest men and women has been done amid great suffering and trial and difficulty.

One of the benefits of adversity is that we're always closer to the Lord during times of trial. He assures us that in Him we can find strength to carry our burdens with ease. We are told to be patient in our afflictions and endure them, for the Lord will be with us "even unto the end of [our] days."[1]

---

1. Doctrine and Covenants 24:8.

Looking beyond Our Sorrows

WE NEED NOT LOOK FAR to see the sorrow and the suffering in the world around us. Scarcely does a week pass, it seems, that we don't witness another calamity that has struck a city, a state, or a nation. Whether it be fire, flood, or war, we can sympathize with the pain that others will endure.

Closer to home, we see too often the sufferings of family, friends, and neighbors. Whether it be a family who has lost a child, a neighbor who is out of work, or a parent who is chronically ill, we likewise see too much pain.

The inevitability of life seems to be that at some point we will bear our share of the world's sorrows. Some may seek to escape them—perhaps through the false security of wealth, through building walls to protect themselves, or through whatever means they believe will keep the world at bay. But those with wisdom know of the need to look beyond what may seem like the hopelessness of the moment.

A young couple whose infant daughter was soon to die had many choices to make during their ordeal, not the least of which was how they would respond to their impending loss. After the doctors had done all they could and it was determined the end would irreversibly present itself, the couple lifted their daughter from her bed, dressed her, and carried her outside for her first and only look at the world. There they basked in the sun for a moment, looked at the flowers and trees, and then returned to the hospital room that had been her only home.

49

With like courage, we should learn to look beyond those times in our lives that appear insurmountable.

We must first look beyond ourselves to those who stand ready to help, to those whose sorrows have passed, to the wisdom left us by wise men and women who have gone before.

And we must look beyond our doubts and fears to those timeless beliefs and values that will help us rise above the difficulties we face.

There is no easy way to circumvent the challenges of life, no foolproof formula that will bring us immediate relief. There is, however, strength to be had in looking beyond the moment—in not losing sight of the hope that there is solace and strength to be found.

All Sunshine Makes the Desert

FROM SOME FORGOTTEN PAGE of mankind's history comes an old saying, its origin lost during generations of use and tradition, but the wisdom of its few words as fresh at truth itself: *"All sunshine makes the desert."*

What does that ancient piece of advice mean to us today? It is to say that an environment where all is positive, an environment where no challenge exists, where sunshine and bliss persist perpetually, is a sterile environment—one devoid of growth and development, a barren desolate place—a desert.

There must be some rain, some darkness, some stormy weather, and contrary winds for life to be rich—for it to become strong and healthy.

One wise religious leader put it this way: "For it must needs be, that there is an opposition in all things."[1] Here, then, is the translation of the proverb: Happiness cannot exist without the possibility of misery; success is meaningless without the potential for failure; intelligence is the corresponding opposite of ignorance; and so on—light and dark, love and hate, life and death.

In its application, the proverb carries with it a practical guide for living, which is that disappointment can be beneficial. Of course, while all sunshine makes the desert, all rain makes the swamp. And, too much disappointment can destroy self-image and hamper personal development; but, in proper proportions, adversity can be a stepping stone rather than a stumbling block.

The business owner, while failing at one venture, develops

skills and perceptions that may help create success at future attempts. The basketball team that has lost one game is often better prepared emotionally and physically than the team that has never known defeat. The caring teacher falls short, though sincerely striving to save a student from illiteracy, but in the attempt gains the experience to keep many others from dropping out.

There is also a lesson here for parents: Parents, do not try to save your children from every disappointment. Maturity and growth result from not getting everything we want—the boy who sits on the bench at Little League once in a while understands the dejection of those who sit out the whole game; the girl who doesn't get new designer clothes every time the fad changes understands a little better what it's like not to be able to afford new clothes. Indeed, gratitude and empathy are products of healthy disappointment and adversity.

So, don't be afraid of a little rain—for all sunshine makes the desert.

---

1. 2 Nephi 2:11.

Acceptance

No MATTER WHO WE ARE or what our station in life may be, trouble comes to us all. It may appear in the guise of financial insecurity or ill health or difficult personal relationship, but— make no mistake—trouble pays each of us a visit. Adversity, in fact, is life's great equalizer.

People respond to adversity in different ways. Some grow angry and bitter, while others despair and even lose hope. But, no matter how we face trouble, most all of us have wished to flee it. Who among us, in the wake of some new misfortune, has not uttered an urgent prayer to the Lord asking Him to lift our latest burden?

Upon learning that her vibrant daughter had been diagnosed with a chronic illness, one mother said to the family's physician, "I hope and pray for a miracle that will take this from her."

After a moment's consideration, the doctor responded, "I see miracles all the time in my work. The miracle isn't always that a condition or an illness disappears, but that families learn to deal with it."

The great American philosopher William James had this to say about dealing with trouble: "Be willing to have it so; acceptance of what has happened is the first step to overcoming the consequences of any misfortune."[1]

Acceptance is the brave act of acknowledging the reality of a situation. The person who practices it may not greet personal troubles with open arms but is wise enough to sit down at the dinner table with them for a good, hard look once they have arrived. Acceptance can be, of course, a difficult art to practice, because it often involves putting aside cherished dreams—like those of a loving mother who desires a life free of medical restrictions for her beautiful daughter.

And yet, in the very act of letting go of what we want and accepting what *is,* there comes an unexpected peace—a sweet peace that fills our hearts and clears our minds—giving us the courage to see new horizons.

And the strength to take fresh steps toward them.

1. In Robert I. Fitzhenry, ed., *The Harper Book of Quotations,* 3rd ed. (New York: HarperCollins Publishers, 1993), p. 17.

Pleasure Mixed with Pain

THERE IS SO MUCH DIVERSITY in our lives—trouble mixed with triumph, pleasure mixed with pain. Sometimes it's possible to ignore the one and focus on the other, to exchange the potential for grief with the opportunity for gladness. But, frequently, we cannot choose. Tragedy or lesser trouble comes; and, in spite of all that is good in our lives, we are overwhelmed by the loss of the moment.

A woman, remembering the death of her father, said, "I couldn't think of any real reason to go on living. Life had become tragic—full of impossible tasks and unbearable consequences. I wandered through our house, seeing only things that reminded me of him, of the life we had shared, of the things we'd never do again." Such monumental loss may make us think the only comfort must have similar size; and, thinking that, we may despair. But the blessing of hope and gladness may come in the smallest moment, the slightest instance of pleasure mixed with pain—which is what this woman discovered. "I found myself in the kitchen," she continued, "and, out of habit, I took a slice of bread from the cupboard, toasted it, buttered it, spread it with raspberry jam bottled and brought over by a neighbor. And, when I took a bite, I was amazed. The nutty taste of whole wheat bread, the mixed, tart sweetness of raspberries—they *still* tasted good. Isn't that amazing?" she wondered. "The taste of bread brought me back; somehow the sweetness of raspberry jam reminded me of the many reasons I have to live."

Raspberry jam and whole wheat bread may not seem like

much; and sometimes it's not so simple nor so possible to overcome the hardship in our lives, to remind ourselves of sweeter moments, happier times, and to find the comfort available to us in even the hardest times. There is no logic that can argue with our hearts or teach us not to suffer for the losses that come with living. But there are comforts that endure even the gravest challenges in our lives; and, when the sun goes down, we can be certain not only that it will rise again, but also that it is shining still, somewhere—that it will shine again for us.

There is whole wheat bread and raspberry jam for us all: opportunities for pleasure in the moment of pain—comfort and comforting that will come from the most unexpected and apparently insignificant sources. Because, after all its grief and losses, life still is good, hopeful. The hope may be hidden from us in times of trouble, but the emblems and evidences of hope are abundant, beckoning to us, asking us to recognize them and be glad. And each of these small moments of gladness can remind us of the larger gladness for which we ultimately hope: the saving grace of Jesus Christ that ultimately surpasses all tragedy and restores all loss, so that, in times of trouble, we also may sing with the psalmist: "Thou hast put gladness in my heart, . . . I will both lay me down in peace, and sleep: for thou, Lord, only makest me dwell in safety."[1]

1. Psalm 4:7–8.

Be Strong and of Good Courage

Imagine Joshua's feelings of fear—and maybe even inadequacy—as he was called to take the place of the great prophet Moses, the man whom he had followed and served for so many years. How comforting the Lord's counsel during that time of transition: "As I was with Moses, so I will be with thee: I will not fail thee, nor forsake thee. Be strong and of a good courage."[1] Those words of divine assurance must have calmed Joshua's heart and bolstered his belief in himself and in his God.

Even so, knowing Joshua's heart and mind—and perhaps sensing some lingering doubt and fear—the Lord reaffirmed: "Have not I commanded thee? Be strong and of good courage; be not afraid, neither be thou dismayed: for the Lord thy God is with thee whithersoever thou goest."[2]

Like Joshua, many of us are called to take on overwhelming responsibilities, even burdens. We all experience changing circumstances and go through unsettling transitions. Such change may be difficult to manage and may even seem impossible or unbearable at moments. We may want to stop the clock, bring back the past, or deny the reality we are forced to face. We may grapple to hold on to what was or what could have been. But life marches on, and with it must come change.

Growth, maturity, and opportunities to demonstrate true devotion accompany such moments of transition. For, as Emerson has written, "Power . . . resides in the moment of transition from a past to a new state, in the shooting of the gulf, in the darting to an aim."[3] It would be easy, or at least painless, to proclaim our faith with no challenge before us: no gulf to cross, no aim for which to dart. Eternal verities would seem so much more acceptable if change—with all of its discomforts and growing pains—were not so relentlessly lurking.

But the strength and courage the Lord promised to Joshua is given to all who faithfully strive. When we humbly go forth, when we honestly attempt, as we patiently and prayerfully try, the Lord will bless us with the power to persist. For those in the midst of transition—for those who feel overwhelmed and inadequate to the task—look to the Lord for support, direction, and security. He knows your heart and your sincere desires. And His message to Joshua over three thousand years ago is the same to us today: "I will not fail thee, nor forsake thee. Be strong and of good courage."

1. Joshua 1:5–6.
2. Joshua 1:9.
3. "Self-Reliance," *The Essays of Ralph Waldo Emerson* (Norwalk, Connecticut: Easton Press, 1979), p. 29.

Only Half a Mile to Go

IT WASN'T THE NUMBING COLD that defeated the former Olympic champion, Florence Chadwick, on that eventful day in 1952, nor the dulling fatigue that had accumulated during fifteen hours of swimming in the currents off Santa Catalina, nor even the lack of endurance—there was still sufficient stamina to complete the last few hundred yards of the twenty-six-mile journey.

But, nonetheless, Florence was hauled from the water less than one-half mile from the shore—a short distance from being the first woman in history to complete the difficult swim from Catalina to the California coast.

No, it wasn't cold or fatigue or weakness that turned success to failure, but lack of vision. Florence couldn't see the shore for the fog. Had she known how close she was to the objective, she would have kept going.

Many of us are like Florence: we have the skill, the motivation, the will to accomplish our goals, but we lose sight of the objective. We let the clutter and debris of life obscure our vision and thus lose sight of our goals.

To her credit, Florence got up to try again. Everything was the same for the second try: the currents were just as strong, the water as cold, the fog as dense as that which had obscured her vision on the first attempt.

All was the same—except for one thing: Florence. This time, she carried with her a mental image of the shore—an image so vivid and detailed that she could envision every rock on the distant coast. And, when she reached the fog bank that had destroyed her faith only two short months before, she swam on. Now she could look through the mist and obscurity. She knew the shore was there because she could see it—not with the naked eye but with the mind's eye. She could envision the image of the goal that she herself had created.

Creating a mental image of our objective is a prime ingredient to success. It's like a road map or blueprint of what we want to accomplish.

The lesson is clear. Through fog and contrary currents, we must hold to our course, keeping a vivid image of our goal in mind, until at last the image becomes reality and the race is won.

Perseverance

THE STORY OF THE LITTLE STEAM ENGINE that said "I think I can!" has inspired children for generations. Its message of perseverance, its example of unstoppable determination has made the "little engine that could" a model for "can-do" thinking. And, from this tale, we construct a parable for life.

Each of us faces obstacles as we climb the hills of life. The challenges come in so many different forms: ill health, meager finances, stressful relationships, and more. Just when all seems to be going well, we run into a roadblock, take a wrong turn, or hit a dead end. Yes, the hard things of life are part of the road we all must travel.

But, like the little engine that could, it takes resolve and perseverance to win uphill battles—nothing less than persistence to see the journey through. Many years ago, a wise but unknown author wrote:

> When things go wrong, as they sometimes will,
> When the road you're trudging seems all up hill,
>
> . . . .
>
> When care is pressing you down a bit,
> Rest, if you must—but don't you quit.[1]

Occasionally, in doing battle with life, it's wise to rest—to pull off to the side of the road and catch our breath—but, all the while, remain doggedly determined, steadfast, and committed to getting up and over the hill.

Perseverance makes up for so many disadvantages and lack of opportunities. Frequently, people who must work harder, study longer, or overcome more, achieve the most significant victories. Success is not always for those of gifted birth, high I.Q., or stunning beauty. More often than not, the difference between people who achieve and those who don't is drive, focus, and a willingness to continue striving. Like the little engine that could, those who come off triumphant are those who keep trying.

Calvin Coolidge wisely said: "Nothing in the world can take the place of persistence. Talent will not. . . . Genius will not. . . . Education will not. . . . Persistence and determination are omnipotent. The slogan 'press on' has solved and always will solve the problems of the human race."[2]

With the words "I think I can!" clearing the way before him, the little steam engine won an uphill battle because he pressed on. Time and again, determination and perseverance bring the victory.

1. "Don't Quit," in Suzy Platt, ed., *Respectfully Quoted: A Dictionary of Quotations Requested from the Congressional Research Service* (Washington: Library of Congress, 1989), p. 255.
2. Ibid.

A Pioneering Spirit

MANY PIONEERS who settled the West did so in pursuit of religious freedom. The Constitution of the United States protected the freedom to worship as they pleased, but some of their neighbors showed little respect for Constitutional guarantees.

So, with faith in God and grateful hearts, the pioneers looked west, where there were fewer neighbors and more freedom to practice their religious beliefs. To them, the West was a promised land. They loaded their possessions in covered wagons and blazed trails across wild prairies and rugged mountains.

Tens of thousands trekked those primitive trails between 1847 and 1869, when the railroad came along to end the early pioneer era. Still, almost every city, town, and hamlet in the West owes its existence to those brave pioneers who first pushed the frontiers of civilization westward.

They were hardy men and women who knew the meaning of work and the satisfaction that comes from honest labor. They knew that only hard work and perseverance would allow them to build settlements in the desert. And they were thankfully aware of each success along the way.

Perhaps that sense of awareness is the most important difference between those pioneers and their modern counterparts. Settling the West was a vital, enriching experience. When they paused for a cool drink of water, it came from a well they themselves had dug. When they rested at the end of a hard day, the light

63

in the room came from candles they themselves had made. When they sat down to a meal, the food came from their own fields.

No wonder these pioneers were so rich with the spirit of thankfulness. They appreciated what they had, and they gave thanks humbly and openly to Divine Providence. In fact, the house of worship was not only the center of most villages, but it was also the main source of support—the glue holding together family and community and nation.

We modern Americans like to believe we are exactly like those early pioneers in courage and resourcefulness and spirituality—perhaps a little wiser, a little more experienced, but molded from the same pioneer stock. We hope the spirit of thankfulness has not faded. We hope the timeless philosophies have not weakened. We hope the urge for independence and freedom has not diminished.

And we are confident that true awareness of life and appreciation for its blessings does not require covered wagons, a barren desert, and a constant struggle merely to survive.

Because we are all pioneers. The scenery changes. The challenges change. But success today requires a pioneer spirit no less than it did in those early days. We may not be crossing a desert, but we, too, must conquer our own complex world. That is our pioneering heritage—and our pioneering challenge.

If we remember well the example of those early pioneers, then we, too, will be able to say with conviction: "All is well! All is well!"

I Wonder If It Will
Turn Out All Right

I WONDER IF IT WILL TURN OUT ALL RIGHT." It is a familiar question. No matter what our age or circumstance, life brings challenges that cause us to wonder if all will be well. In our era, the uncertainties include global concerns about warfare, pollution, safety, finances, and family stability. The rapid changes in technology and lifestyle can also make us occasionally feel off balance. The daily news can make us pause, questioning if anything can be well in such a time as ours—a world replete with emotional turmoil, strident voices, and economic woes.

For most of us, the concerns that puzzle us are far more personal. A father frets over a feverish child. A teenager worries about his performance in the school play. A new employee anxiously begins her first day on the job. A grandmother lies awake at night, worrying about the surgery she faces. In these and hundreds of daily situations, we wonder if it will turn out all right.

Others living in equally stressful times have left us words of counsel. The prophet Moses reminded his people, "Be strong and of a good courage."[1] Many stabilizing influences give us reason to move forward with strength and courage. Spring comes, usually on schedule, handing all of us a garland of blossoms that reminds us how beautiful the world can be. Graduation launches a new generation of eager youth into the world. A child learns to walk, showing us how much we have already learned. A wedding anniversary validates the strength of loving commitments. A community group cleans a busy highway, investing their time and labor in a common good.

These daily events quietly demonstrate that we have reason to feel things can be made well and to live with courage. Through these simple occurrences, we find hope for our communities, faith in the essential goodness of most of our fellow travelers on earth, joy in our own families and friends.

We may worry about the uncertainty of our days, but we have many reasons to be strong and courageous. The ordinary acts of good people encourage us to believe that everything will turn out all right.

1. Deuteronomy 31:6.

Take No Thought for the Morrow

Today is the tomorrow you worried about yesterday." Such popular wisdom reminds us that, no matter how much we stew over tomorrow's concerns, each day gives way to another new day and will never bring back yesterday. Instead of feeling threatened by the passage of time, we can be comforted that "the world passeth away . . . but he that doeth the will of God abideth forever."[1]

When we remember that "our light affliction . . . is but for a moment,"[2] we allow the perspective of eternity to ease the problems of humanity. Our worries become less significant as we replace fear with faith and idleness with sincere and directed effort. We must use our time to tackle present problems and not waste our precious resources worrying about past mistakes and possible failures. Worry saps our energy and leaves us anxious and frustrated. For as long as life is less than perfect, there will always be things to worry about.

Richard L. Evans so wisely observed: "Often we worry about arriving at an end, with too little faith in what follows. In any year, in any day, we are given to worrying about much that has happened, much that hasn't happened, much that doesn't happen. With problems, with disappointments, and sometimes in sorrow, the question comes to troubled hearts: 'What am I going to do now?' The answer inevitably is, continue to do what needs to be done, what can be done; to do the necessary things, and have the faith to know that life will unfold, as it always has, as it continues to do."[3]

Time *is* on our side. As life unfolds, we can be grateful that each day evolves into a new day; each heartache, each pain, each challenge is only temporary. Because the Lord assures us that our suffering is "but for a moment," we can stop worrying, start working, and really enjoy the journey of life.

God did not give us the breath of life that we might inhale distress and exhale anxiety. Instead, we can take the deep breath of determination, start each day with a fresh outlook, and renew our resolve to go forward with faith. In the Lord's own words: "Take . . . no thought for the morrow: for the morrow shall take thought for the things of itself."[4] Each day is full of opportunity and blessing. Today is the day to leave our worries behind and look for the good that can be done, the burdens that can be lifted, the positive efforts that can be made.

1. 1 John 2:17.
2. 2 Corinthians 4:17.
3. *May Peace Be With You* (New York: Harper & Brothers, 1961), p. 235.
4. Matthew 6:34.

The Welcoming
Door of Optimism

Habits of thinking and patterns of believing have consequences. The way we look at the world, in large measure, shapes
the kind of life we will have. Do we see potential and possibility—
or do we dwell on defeat and despair? Do we recognize opportunity and blessings—or are we blinded by what seems to be "bad
luck"? Shakespeare has written, "There is nothing either good or
bad but thinking makes it so."[1] How we think and what we believe
literally determine the amount of good or bad that we find within
us and around us.

Hundreds of studies show that optimists perform more productively than pessimists. Even when facing the same unfavorable
circumstances, optimists persist in well-doing. They do much better in school and at work; their health is better—they may even
live longer.[2] Optimists believe that tomorrow will come, circumstances will improve, solutions will be discovered, and that somehow it'll all work out. They believe that life is basically good, and
they give thanks to God for the blessings—and even the challenges—of life.

Pessimists, on the other hand, are always aware of what's
wrong, what could be better, and what hasn't worked in the past.
They feel as though they were born to fail and believe that, if there
is a God, He must have forgotten about them. Unlike the

Pollyanna, who makes a game out of being glad, they may look for reasons to be unhappy.

Real optimism, however, centers on a deep and abiding faith in ourselves and in God. What many of us call optimism was more accurately known as faith by the prophets of old. Paul demonstrated such belief when he proclaimed to the Philippians: "I can do all things through Christ which strengtheneth me."[3] That very ability to move mountains, to part the Red Sea, and to make water spring forth from a dry rock takes root in the hopeful and expectant thoughts of the optimist.

The Lord can give us the power to move mountains of trouble in our lives, to part seas of discouragement, and to moisten the hardness of human hearts when we are exercising faith by first thinking positively. It's never easy, and it's seldom luck. But real strength comes from allowing God into our lives through the welcoming door of optimism.

1. *Hamlet,* act 2, scene 3, lines 255–56.
2. Information taken from Martin E. F. Seligman, *Learned Optimism* (New York: Alfred A. Knopf, 1991), pp. 3–16.
3. Philippians 4:13.

The Hope of Spring

....

ALL SEEMS HOPEFUL and happy at the advent of spring. A winter-weary world breathes a sigh of relief. Birds sing triumphant songs as they return to blossoming trees. Flowers put on their victory colors after conquering the cold, hardened earth. And children gladly take off their winter coats—free to roam, laugh, and play in the beauty and brightness of the season.

But, as we all know, a harsh cold front is never too far away during this time of transition. The wind may suddenly pick up, the air turn cold, and the snow start to fall—just when we least expect it. Old Man Winter may return with a vengeance—suffocating flowers with frost, sending birds to search for shelter, and forcing children back indoors.

Eventually, spring will return to stay—and with it the steadiness of summer. But, for a time, its beauty is tenuous, even while its promise is sure: winter will pass and the earth will be renewed to springtime glory.

This cycle of change and rejuvenation gives us hope and reminds us of the new life promised to all. Just as surely as one season evolves into the next, the challenges of earth life can give way to the celebration of eternal life. The Lord provided the way: "I am the resurrection, and the life: he that believeth in me, though he were dead, yet shall he live."[1]

In the middle of winter, we may wonder if spring will ever come—and stay. And, in the winters of our discontent, when the storms of our sojourn seem to blow without relent, we can pray for the peaceful assurance of a better day. Job's reasoning of centuries past can still our minds: "There is hope of a tree, if it be cut down, that it will sprout again, and that the tender branch thereof will not cease. Though the roof . . . wax old in the earth, and the stock . . . die in the ground; yet through the scent of water it will bud, and bring forth boughs like a plant."[2]

The renewal of spring is a model for our promise of eternal life. When the harsh, cold elements combine, when the burdens seem too much to bear, know that spring will come. The frozen earth will give way to beautiful flowers of faith, the silence of cold air will be broken by a bird's song of hope, the stillness of winter's landscape will be enlivened by precious children. Each season in the cycle of renewal gives us the hope of new life and fuels our faith in the advent of an everlasting spring.

1. John 11:25.
2. Job 14:7–9.

Looking Up

"LOOK FOR THE SILVER LINING" hearkens back to the motto of the Lend a Hand Society, formed over a hundred years ago by Edward Everett Hale:

> Look up and not down;
> Look forward and not back;
> Look out and not in;
> Lend a Hand.[1]

This short creed outlines an abundant approach to life—a positive personal outlook and a kind regard for all people.

"Look up and not down; look forward and not back" is a simple yet profound formula for happiness. To look for the good, we must look up to God. Faith will help us find the silver lining in even the darkest cloud, to focus on the good when life's challenges would get us down. Regardless of how dismal our circumstances may seem today, we can look to a brighter tomorrow. Everything always seems a little better in the light of morning sun.

The fact is, we tend to find exactly what we look for. Whether in other people, ourselves, the day, or life in general, faithful optimists discover the good, the praiseworthy, the kindnesses all around them. They understand that the past cannot be redone, so they live with zest for today and look forward to the promise of tomorrow. Such positive resiliency makes each new day more meaningful, more hopeful. Although it is not always easy, the courageous believer looks up and moves forward.

"Look out and not in; Lend a Hand," the motto concludes. Who among us does not welcome a helping hand? Likewise, who hasn't felt the joy of giving service? The interdependent nature of our lives means we need each other. And we all have something to give: sometimes it may be time, other times attention, maybe our means, and always kindness. By focusing on others, their worries and concerns, their questions and interests, we shift our orientation from self and feel the satisfaction of reaching out. Whether a phone call, a visit, a letter, or a pat on the back, looking out for others is the essence of positive and abundant living.

One young man began to realize the importance of looking up and moving on after a serious personal loss. With many years still ahead of him, he could choose happiness or he could settle for disappointment and sadness. He chose to be a faithful optimist, daily striving to lend a hand and ever looking to God for strength. He gave generously of his limited resources and lived by the light of another inspiring creed: Pain is inevitable, but misery is optional. "By having faith and helping others, I can choose to be happy," he reminded himself. This precious perspective has made all the difference in his life.

Regardless of our situation, we can decide now to "Look up and not down; look forward and not back; look out and not in; lend a Hand."

1. In Suzy Platt, ed., *Respectfully Quoted: A Dictionary of Quotations Requested from the Congressional Research Service* (Washington: Library of Congress, 1989), p. 268.

PART 3

The Peace
of God's Gifts

"Not As the World Giveth"

THE HALLMARK OF JESUS' LIFE was peace. Peace was the word at His birth; and a brief thirty-three years later, as His apostles gathered together for a last supper with Him, peace was again the promise He gave them.

How grieved these men must have felt to know that their dearest friend would soon be taken from them in such a cruel way. How heavy their spirits as Christ said to them, "Little children, yet a little while I am with you. . . . Whither I go, ye cannot come."[1]

But He left them a promise: "Peace I leave with you, my peace I give unto you: not as the world giveth, give I unto you."[2] Peace at His birth, peace at His death—peace given, He says, to all those who will abide in Him.

Why, then, do we have so little peace? On a global level, we hold our peace talks and still peace eludes us. In our own hearts, peace often eludes us, too. If we had peace within, there would not be so much anger, jealousy, and fear. We would not quarrel with one another, hold on to offenses, seek to take advantage of one another. We would not need to prove we were right; we would not need to win. All this unrest among us shows how deeply our hearts are in turmoil.

Peace, we suppose, is for another time when we have less to do, fewer voices demanding our attention, fewer pressures. It is for a time when the irritants have been removed from our lives, when we feel better about ourselves, when we don't have to cope with loss or grief or tragedy. Perhaps, it is for a day when we can take a few hours for ourselves for a walk alone in the country. Surely, there is a quiet place where our blood will stop pounding and we can feel in touch again with ourselves.

These are all false solutions. Why do we search in the world for something the world can never offer? The Lord said that what He gave was "not as the world giveth." It is a peace that "passeth all understanding"[3] because it is not attached to anything here. It is not a product of free time or material security; it is not even a product of a life without trial. It is His gift, and only He can give it.

We have sometimes seen this peace on the face of parents who have lost their precious child; heard it on the lips of a prophet going to be martyred; felt it in our souls, even when our world seems to be crumbling down about us. It is a peace that calms a troubled heart and quiets fears. It says, "Be still, and know that I am God."[4] Is anything impossible for the Lord?

It is no accident that the Lord came to give us this peace, for without it our lives are a tangle of unmet needs, and we run through life always looking but never finding that thing that will finally give us comfort. His life and His promise to all this is so simple. Abide in Him, and He will give what this world cannot give. It is peace.

1. John 13:33.
2. John 14:27.
3. Philippians 4:7.
4. Psalm 46:10.

Knowing the Father

So many things about our lives are unknowable. We set career goals and plan vacations and look to the future. We have confidence that we can anticipate what will happen, that we can depend on the events of the present to endure into the future and create a world we can count on.

But we can't count on the world. We never could. No matter what we plan, the world will change. Tragedy may take us unaware, regardless of what we accomplish; undeserved failure may diminish and undo our lives. As a result, those of us who set our hearts on the accomplishments of the world will discover the world to be fickle and unreliable.

But, if we can't count on this world with its tangible, knowable events and uncertain rewards, what can we count on?

Revealed religion has always told us we can count on God. But, while the disadvantage of the world is its unreliability, religious skeptics argue that the disadvantage of God is that He is unknowable—too far away to be of practical help. Even if we hope to go to heaven, the skeptic says, how does that help with the pain we feel now; the sense of loss we feel for the failure in our lives; the terror we feel when alone at night? In other words, if the sink is leaking in the kitchen, how does it help to know that God is our Father?

Well, if the help we most need is fixing a leaky sink, we may need a plumber more than a prayer. But, while prayer may not help the sink, it can help us. Because prayer helps us to *know*—not the practical knowledge of this world, but the more enduring knowledge of eternal worlds: the knowledge that God is our Father; that He feels our pain; that, in the darkest nights when no light may come, He knows us and loves us and pities us for the darkness we endure.

Even when there is no help to fix the leaky sink, prayer can see us through the failures, help us persevere past the pain. There is no way to avoid the trouble and disappointment of living. Part of the reason we are here is to suffer the pains of life, to experience the trouble and travail of this world.

What gives us the will to survive is not necessarily solutions to our problems but companionship for our grief: the sharing of loved ones, the love of God. And, when there is no other comfort strong enough, God is strong. And, where there is no other love long enough, God's love is long—eternal. The world is easier to see, more confident to touch; but God is the giver whose gifts endure. He is our Father. And, even when He seems so far away, He is near—hoping to help us, eager to touch us, longing to comfort us with His love.

The Gift of Life

LIFE IS SUCH A UNIVERSAL GIFT that it is sometimes easy to take for granted—to stop seeing all of the wonders that characterize our existence. We may be so busy making a living that we fail to design a life. We may get so involved in improving our lifestyle that we lose sight of the simple pleasures that come from just living.

Norman Vincent Peale contrasts our lives today with those of our forefathers. They seemed to be more aware of the preciousness (and precariousness) of life, because their living was so closely aligned with the passing of the seasons, the cycles of planting and harvesting, of being born and of dying. Whereas, "we have become the children of cities. We live in the midst of concrete and steel. We are beset on every side with evidence, not of God's creation, but of man's handiwork. And we have become a little smug and sophisticated with it all. We have forgotten our own mortality."[1]

When we are aware that life is a gift from God, that there is a reason for our being, and that life does not end when death opens its door, we see power and purpose all around us—and within us: we feel the summer's heat and know of the Lord's refining fire; we are chilled by the snows of winter and become grateful that death has lost its sting;[2] we recognize the first buds of spring as evidence of our eternal life and see the first fruits of the harvest as symbols of a life well lived.

It is sometimes hard to believe what we cannot see—to trust

in the promise of eternal life when our present is so pressing. But even the heaviest sorrows and prolonged adversities cannot shut out the "Light of the World" and keep us from enjoying the beauties around us. In fact, some of our most painful experiences will lead us to discover greater light, to search for meaning in our existence, to appreciate the gift of life.

As William Penn observed, "The truest end of life is to know the Life that never ends."[3] Or, in the Savior's own words, "Whosoever liveth and believeth in me shall never die."[4] When we know that our Redeemer lives, we do not as readily take for granted God's gifts, the greatest of which is more precious even than life itself—the gift of everlasting life.

1. *Plus, the Magazine of Positive Thinking,* April 1992, p. 4.
2. 1 Corinthians 15:55.
3. In Richard L. Evans, *Richard Evans' Quote Book* (Salt Lake City, Utah: Publisher's Press, 1971), p. 118.
4. John 11:26.

Living with Purpose

Aᴛ ᴏɴᴇ ᴘᴏɪɴᴛ ᴏʀ ᴀɴᴏᴛʜᴇʀ, we may all take a good, long look in the mirror and ask, "Who am I?" and "Why am I here on earth?" Such penetrating questions lead us to search for the universal purpose of life and our individual reason for being. These simple, basic, and timeless ponderings are at the heart of human existence. And, when these fundamental questions are answered with the understanding of our eternal relationship with God—as His children—we are molded into unique persons with divinely inspired purposes.

We are not pawns on some celestial chessboard—arbitrarily put here, tossed about, and expected to figure out for ourselves the "game" of life. As children of a loving God, we each have purpose, destiny, and reason for being. We each have unique abilities and individualized strengths. For example, a fish is as unique as a camel. But don't expect a fish to survive the Sahara, nor a camel to swim the Atlantic. You are as unique as the person sitting next to you.

The fact that we can discover our distinct purposes, make correct choices, and realize our individual missions in life empowers us with the energy and humility we need to persevere. When we know that God created us and sent us to earth, we have greater energy to fulfill the measure of our creation. When we humble ourselves enough to recognize our dependence upon God—our need for a Heavenly Father—we can more readily accept and more diligently work toward such meaningful living.

The Peace of God's Gifts

We are alive, and we are here on earth because there is a God in heaven who loves us—and who knows us individually. He said of His own handiwork, "As the clay is in the potter's hand, so are ye in mine hand."[1] On a daily basis, we can be molded; we can change; and we can look to Him for purpose. We can, with meekness and humility, seek to do His will; or we can, with pride and arrogance, refuse to be molded by His perfectly loving and knowing hand.

David O. McKay has summarized: "Sculptors of life are we with our uncarved souls before us. Every one of us is carving a soul. Is it going to be a deformed one or is it going to be a thing of beauty?"[2] And beautiful it will be when we discover the power of purposeful living—when we know who we really are and why we came to earth.

....

1. Jeremiah 18:6.
2. In Francis M. Gibbons, *David O. McKay* (Salt Lake City: Deseret Book Co., 1986), p. 288.

Pieces of the Puzzle

THIS LAND—AND THIS LIFE—ARE LIKE JIGSAW PUZZLES, each piece fitting into the whole with its unique and distinct design. No one piece is just like another; and yet, all of the parts work toward the same end. Each of us lives interdependently with one another: doing our part, sharing common borders, and following guidelines set for us. Although we each have a piece of the puzzle, none of us has it all. Only God is the Holder of all the pieces—the Definer of all the parts—and His hope and command is that we become like Him.

Even so, He has said to us, "Thou mayest choose for thyself."[1] What we do with our portion of the puzzle is a function of our God-given agency. He would have us reach to our limits, smooth out our rough edges, and fill in the empty spaces. Because He can see the whole picture, God knows better than we do what we have the power to become. He knows the potential of each of us and, as a perfect and loving Father, would not be content with anything less than sincere and consistent improvement.

The Lord meant what He said when He gave the command: "Be ye therefore perfect, even as your Father which is heaven is perfect."[2] While the Lord knew that the process would be long and difficult, His words bear testimony of our ultimate potential for good. The great Christian writer and Oxford professor, C. S. Lewis, wrote: "The command 'Be ye perfect' is not idealistic gas. . . . He is going to make good His words. If we let Him—for we can prevent Him if we choose—He will make the feeblest . . . of us into . . . a dazzling, radiant, immortal creature, pulsating all through with such energy and joy and wisdom and love as we cannot now imagine."[3]

God is the great Architect, the grand designer of this life. And the more we follow His plan for us, turning to Him for direction and vision, the better we will understand our unique piece of life's eternal puzzle. You and I can discover God's great intentions for us and—with patience for the process of life, a teachable spirit, and a desire to serve Him—build a place in His kingdom.

1. Moses 3:17.
2. Matthew 5:48.
3. C. S. Lewis, *Mere Christianity* (New York: Macmillan, 1952), pp. 173–74.

Earth in Its Glory

H ERE WE ARE, living and breathing on this beautiful planet, usually not even realizing that its glorious mass is suspended in space. We witness the changing of the seasons, the rotation of the earth, the great and small wonders of this world with every rising and falling of the sun. And yet, sometimes we fail to see the hand of God in it all.

The psalmist observed, "The heavens declare the glory of God; and the firmament sheweth his handywork."[1] And we, too, would be wise to recognize the earth's demonstration of divinity. John Milton was humbled by the majesty of it all:

> When I behold thy Heavens, thy Fingers art
> The Moon and Starrs which thou so bright hast set,
> In the pure firmament, then saith my heart,
> O what is man that thou remembrest yet,
> And think'st upon him?[2]

Think a moment on the organization and operation of it all: the temperature that sustains life; the balance of land, water, and air; the plants, animals, fish, and insects in all their diversity; and the human being, who is unsurpassed by them all.

As incomprehensibly grand as are the creations of earth and space, there is no creation as precious, even as sacred, as that of man and woman. "In the beginning God created the heaven and the earth. . . . And God saw every thing that he had made, and, behold, it was very good."[3] But "God created man in his own image, in the image of God created he him; male and female created he them."[4] While all of God's creations are pleasing to Him, all of us were created in His image. Could there be a more exalting and refining truth than that all of us are literally His children? Our lives can take on new meaning as we realize the certainty of our divine creation, of our inherent worth, of our likeness to Him.

For those who wonder about the existence of God, the world speaks of His glory. For those who are fearful and frustrated—for those who doubt their own worth—you are God's most glorious creation. He knows you. He loves you. Just as the earth bespeaks God's greatness, the human mind, body, and spirit tell of His infinite goodness—His Fatherly providence.

1. Psalm 19:1.
2. Psalm VIII, in Mortimer J. Adler, ed., *Great Books of the Western World* (Chicago: Encyclopaedia Britannica, 1990), 29:167.
3. Genesis 1:1, 31.
4. Genesis 1:27.

The Temple of God

We love thy house, O God,
Wherein thine honor dwells.
The joy of thine abode
All earthly joy excels.[1]

THROUGH THE AGES, God-fearing people have built temples. The tabernacle of Moses, the temple of Solomon, and the sanctuaries of today are sacred and holy places of worship. Places of spiritual healing. Places of reverence and devotion to the Most High. As the psalmist has written, "Who shall ascend into the hill of the Lord? or who shall stand in his holy place? He that hath clean hands, and a pure heart."[2] For as long as men and women have worshiped in holy places, hands and hearts have been washed clean, heads and knees bowed, eyes and lips stilled in preparation for sacred service.

The Apostle Paul wrote of another kind of temple—a temple constructed not of stone and mortar but of flesh and bone. "Know ye not that ye are the temple of God," he wrote, "and that the Spirit of God dwelleth in you?"[3] This question has echoed in our halls of worship for centuries, but has it found place in our hearts? If we were to think of our family members, friends, and associates as temples would they be deserving of better care, more compassionate treatment, and greater respect? Would our hands be clean and our hearts pure in relation to other people? If we really saw each other as holy houses wherein God's honor dwells, would we be more willing to serve, sacrifice, and even believe in one another?

The American philosopher Ralph Waldo Emerson thought so. "A man is the facade of a temple," he explained, "wherein all wisdom and all good abide. What we commonly call man, the eating, drinking, planting, counting man, does not, as we know him, represent himself. . . . Him we do not respect, but the soul, whose organ he is, would he let it appear through his action, would make our knees bend."[4]

In other words, just as temples made of stone are holy houses, all of God's children—no matter how exalted or humble—house within themselves a sacred spirit. Do we recognize—and revere—these sanctuaries all around us?

These are worthy of respect, honor, and love as surely as are the earthly temples of stone and mortar that we cherish.

> Behold, the tabernacle of God is with men,
> And the spirit of God dwelleth within you:
> For the temple of God is holy,
> Which temple ye are.[5]

1. "We Love Thy House, O God," *Hymns of The Church of Jesus Christ of Latter-day Saints* (Salt Lake City: The Church of Jesus Christ of Latter-day Saints, 1985), no. 247.

2. Psalm 24:3, 4.

3. 1 Corinthians 3:16.

4. "The Over-Soul," *The Essays of Ralph Waldo Emerson* (Norwalk, Connecticut: Easton Press, 1979), p. 108.

5. "Behold, the Tabernacle of God," from the Sarum Antiphon (Royal School of Church Music).

God's Wondrous Creations

ABANDONING THE HECTIC RHYTHMS of the city and suburb, Anne Morrow Lindbergh went alone to the seashore. Feeling desperate need to bring balance into her life, she wrote: "Here there is time; time to be quiet, time to work without pressure; time to think; . . . time to look at the stars or to study a shell."[1] She found the balance she was seeking. She found peace of mind as she pondered on the meaning and wonder of God's creations.

There is evidence of God's wondrous creations all around us. His majesty is witnessed in the pounding of the waves on a rocky shore. His glory is reflected in the rising of the sun signaling the beginning of a bright new day. And what of the symphonies of sound in the air? They are His creation, too. The wind in the trees, the call of a bird, the patter of rain, crickets at night.

No tickets are needed for great performances such as these. Admission is free for those who have eyes to see and ears to hear.

And yet, many of us may close our eyes and ears to the beauty nature has to offer. The loud, insistent music of today drowns out the subtle sounds of the natural world. There is no time in busy schedules for quiet contemplation.

Must it always be so?

We can turn off the music. We don't need to be near an ocean or on a mountaintop to observe God's handiwork. Among His gifts, we have the sky. How long has it been since you watched lazy clouds float along in a sea of blue—or rain clouds sweep across a valley? When did you last take note of a patch of blue in an overcast sky? How long has it been since you counted stars at night and wondered what was beyond them? For many, the answer might be, "Not since I was a child."

Ralph Waldo Emerson said, "All I have seen teaches me to trust the Creator for all I have not seen."[2]

In the beginning, God created the heaven and the earth. He brought the waters together and created the seas. He created the mountains and trees and flowers and every living thing upon the face of the earth. And, when the earth was finished, He created man and woman to enjoy His wondrous creations and to have dominion over them.[3]

Maybe it's time to open our eyes more fully to the beauties of God's creations—time to listen more closely to the sounds of His world and let His peace fill our souls.

1. *Gift from the Sea* (New York: Vintage, 1978), p. 116.
2. In Richard L. Evans, *Richard Evans' Quote Book* (Salt Lake City, Utah: Publisher's Press, 1971), p. 127.
3. Genesis, chapter 1.

The Visible Works of God

SOME FOUR HUNDRED YEARS AGO, the German astronomer Johannes Kepler accurately described the revolutions of the planets around the sun. His mathematical statements, known as "Kepler's Laws," are studied even today. But, according to Kepler, his life's labor was more than a scientific study. In his own words, he was exploring "the visible works of God."

His life was devoted to explaining what he called "the principle parts of the world." And among those parts was light. He wrote, "For as regards light: since the sun is very beautiful with light and is as if the eye of the world, like a source of light or very brilliant torch, the sun illuminates, paints, and adorns the bodies of the rest of the world."[1] Kepler's unusual description of the sun, "as if the eye of the world"—the center of the universe—tells of his deeper understanding.

As the body around which the planets revolve, as the principal source of light and life-giving warmth, the sun is a symbol of the Lord's vital role in sustaining spiritual life. Not only do we need earthly light and warmth from the sun, but our souls also depend upon the heavenly light, warmth, and direction that come from the Son of God: the Light of the World who can illuminate and adorn our lives.[2]

God-fearing believers have recognized this need through the ages. The psalmist wrote—thousands of years before Kepler—of God's purposeful creation: "The day is thine, the night also is thine: thou hast prepared the light and the sun."[3] And David rejoiced: "The Lord is my light and my salvation; whom shall I fear?"[4]

In days of darkness and trouble, it's comforting to know that light is available—that the Lord can be our Light. Sometimes our world looks bleak and gloomy, the sun only a pale reflection of what was, or could be. But through the nocturnal pitch comes the shine of moonlight—for even the night's moon shines light. And, with the light of a new day, the sparkle of hope continues. One more day to live, to contribute, to enjoy. A day to lift someone's burden, to work, to laugh, to pray. That glimmer of light illuminates our lives with fervent hope and scatters the thick darkness of despair. Light gives us life.

Let us thank God for the light and for the Light of the World so that we—like Kepler—can see the sun, moon, and stars as "the visible works of God."

1. Johannes Kepler, "Epitome of Copernican Astronomy: IV and V," in *Great Books of the Western World*, edited by Robert Maynard Hutchins (Chicago: Encyclopaedia Britannica, 1982), 16:854–55.
2. John 8:12.
3. Psalm 74:16.
4. Psalm 27:1.

The Renewing Power of Nature

> O there is blessing in this gentle breeze . . .
> From the green fields, and from yon azure sky.[1]

So BEGINS WILLIAM WORDSWORTH'S EPIC POEM *The Prelude.* Gentle breezes, green fields, azure skies, and mountain vistas inspired this poem and many other great works in literature and life. Captivating scenes from nature somehow elevate thoughts and renew spirits. For Wordsworth, the rural setting of his childhood was the stimulus for much of his poetry. Something about fresh air, the beautiful views, and the remarkable sounds and smells of nature set poetry in motion.

Wordsworth was not alone in his affinity for the natural world. Nature's call to verse has been answered by many a poet and songwriter. Perhaps even more common is the inspiration we each can feel when in the hills, under the stars, surrounded by wildflowers, or near a babbling brook. These simple reminders of God's love for us are what we call nature. And to natural settings we ascribe many of our most meaningful moments and ideas: the sunset that motivates a kiss, the flower that speaks forgiveness, the tree that tells of family ties, and the rock upon which reason is balanced with feeling. We may all dip our hands in the stream of understanding that flows through the heart of nature.

But why does it have such an effect on us? How can we be so inspired by the mountain air, the meadow's color, the streamlet's sound? Perhaps because nature puts our human accomplishments into perspective and gets us to look heavenward. The motion picture of nature needs no lists of credits. The sound of brook, bird, and insect has only one composer. The arrangements of earth and sky know only one artist. For "the heavens declare the glory of God; and the firmament sheweth his handywork."[2]

1. Book 1, lines 1–2.
2. Psalm 19:1.

And the Cock Crows

IT WAS NOON, and the visitor to Israel sat upon the brow of the hill just above the Garden of Gethsemane. Then, unexpectedly, a cock crowed—an unusual sound for midday. It set our visitor to thinking about another time and place not far from there when a cock had crowed in Jerusalem.

At the last supper, just before Christ was tried and condemned to crucifixion, He warned His apostles, "All ye shall be offended because of me this night,"[1]—to which Peter exclaimed with heartfelt emotion, "Though all men shall be offended because of thee, yet will I never be offended."[2] Christ answered: that very night Peter would deny Him three times before the cock crowed signaling the dawn.

Then, in what must have been Peter's most difficult moments, standing outside the palace where Jesus was being tried, he did deny his Lord—denied that he knew Him, denied that he had been with Him. Peter, of course, was chagrined and repentant, and the Savior forgave him. But how tempting it is for all of us, in our own way, to deny the Savior, to be offended by His goodness to us.

Our visitor upon the hill in Jerusalem wondered about this as the cock crowed. "Have I, too, denied the Savior? Have I failed to understand the magnificence of His gift for me?" In Gethsemane, the Savior took upon Himself our pains, groaned in anguish and exquisite pain as He bowed under the sins of the world—this that we would not have to suffer if we would repent.

97

He took upon Himself our sorrows, our burdens, our sickness and anxiety. All we must do is give them to Him, count Him as our Savior, acknowledge His great gift. But the temptation is the same for us as it was for Peter. The temptation is to deny that gift.

We think repentance is for someone else—the really bad guys, the obvious sinners. This is not so. It is for us—that we might have lifted from us all the weaknesses, the pettiness, the fraud, the self-adulation that destroy our happiness. We can be made new. We do not have to carry any of the shackles from yesterday that have kept us from soaring. We do not have to cower before life because we have disappointed ourselves. Because of His great gift to us, the Lord forgives and He forgets.

On the third day after Christ's crucifixion, He arose, His lifeless body resurrected and renewed. Later, on the shores of the Sea of Galilee, Peter was able to affirm three times to Christ what he before had denied. Jesus asked him, "Lovest thou me?"[3] And Peter answered, "Yea, Lord; thou knowest that I love thee,"[4] with unflinching firmness, and he gave his life to show he meant it.

It is Christ's gift to us that both our bodies and our hearts are made new in Him.

1. Matthew 26:31.
2. Matthew 26:33.
3. John 21:16.
4. Ibid.

Living Water

IN THE THIRSTY MONTHS OF SUMMER, we are sometimes dramatically reminded of how dependent we are on water. In fact, the story of life is the story of water. Drive across the country, and you need no meteorologist to tell you how much water any land receives. It is written in the lushness of the growth. A desert is a desert because it has so little rain; it could bloom as a garden with a little water. We ourselves cannot go many hours without water before our mouths are dry and we yearn to drink.

It was surely with these thoughts in mind that a ninety-two-year-old man first visited a great natural spring that gushed forth from the earth with a hundred million gallons of water a day. He had to bring water from the mountains for his crops to grow, and he shook his head at the roar of the spring. "Imagine," he said, "a desert boy like me seeing a scene like this."

It was to a desert people in Israel that the Lord first came, and that setting gives meaning to His invitation, "Come, my brethren, every one that thirsteth, come ye to the waters; and he that hath no money, come buy and eat; yea, come buy wine and milk without money and without price."[1]

We need not thirst, He tells us. In this world of disappointment and pain, where even our best hopes fail us and our mouths are dry and our tongues are swollen, He tells us that He has a gift for us—freely given without price. It is a spring of water that will never run dry. It is His love and protection that is constant. It is His promise of an abundant life.

The Peace of God's Gifts

We are used to a world where things cost us dearly, where things run out, where we struggle by the sweat of our brow for bread. We are used to asking, "How much? How much will it cost me to have my needs met?" It is almost incomprehensible for us to understand that the Lord's gifts are freely given when we turn to receive them.

"Come, my brethren, every one that thirsteth,"[2] He says. And who among us does not?

When the woman of Samaria came to the well to draw water, she was thirsty—in both a physical and spiritual way. She needed water; but, more, she needed home. Her life had been a miserable experience of failed expectations and disappointments, lost marriages and broken laws. It was to her, not to an influential member of the community, the Savior chose to speak. His gift was even available to her. He said, "Whosoever drinketh of the water that I shall give him shall never thirst; but the water that I shall give him shall be in him a well of water springing up into everlasting life."[3]

That same promise is given to all of us—to those of us who wander in the desert with parched souls of sin, sorrow, disappointment, and despair—thirsting after truth and peace and hope. His gift to us is the promise of everlasting water—His love, His gift, His forgiveness, His spirit. That is a wonderful promise to all of us in this life who travel so often in the desert.

1. 2 Nephi 9:50.
2. Ibid.
3. John 4:14.

Miraculous Communication

WE LIVE IN A WORLD filled with unparalleled means of communication. We have television, radio, fax machines, telephones, and computer modems—each sending communication signals at a speed of over 186,000 miles per second. At this rate, my voice, transmitted over the air waves, can travel completely around the world before the same sound waves would reach the rear of this Tabernacle. As astonishing as this technology may be, the most miraculous and dependable communication has been with us since the beginning of time:

> More things are wrought by prayer
> Than this world dreams of. Wherefore, let thy voice
> Rise like a fountain for me night and day.[1]

So wrote Alfred Lord Tennyson.

Yes, the greatest miracle of all communication is the power of prayer. It's a privilege God has given each of us to communicate directly with Him. And, because of His great love for us, He has set no limitation as to when, where, and what we should pray about. As the Apostle Paul wrote, "In every thing by prayer and supplication with thanksgiving let your requests be made known unto God."[2]

Exercising our privilege to pray is an essential ingredient to finding joy and happiness in today's world. Dr. Alexis Carrel has written, "Only in prayer do we achieve that complete and harmonious assembly of body, mind and spirit which gives the frail human its unshakable strength."[3]

Although not every prayer receives a dramatic answer, every simple plea is heard and quietly responded to. Sincere and humble prayer can guide us to a path that leads to peace in this life and eternal life in the world to come.

Yes, we live in a world that offers the technology to quickly communicate information as never before, but the most important line of communication is still between ourselves and God. And, because of His love for us, He promises that line will never be busy.

1. "The Passing of Arthur," *Idylls of the King*, quoted in *The Oxford Dictionary of Quotations* (New York: Oxford University Press, 1992), p. 682.

2. Philippians 4:6.

3. In Ernest R. Miller, ed., *Harvest of Gold* (Norwalk, Conn.: C. R. Gibson, 1973), p. 77.

The Rock of Ages

Rock of Ages, cleft for me, let me hide myself in thee."[1] This beautiful hymn, written more than two hundred years ago, is a familiar favorite. Most of us have either heard it sung, or sung it ourselves, in a variety of worship services. The melody proclaims the majesty of the message. But have we ever paused to think about the meaning of its poetic phrases? Have we ever stopped to make this very personal hymn our own?

"Rock of Ages." A symbol of strength and stability, the *Rock* in this song—and throughout scripture—refers to Deity: a sure foundation upon which to build. When we center our lives on the Rock of our Salvation, we will be able to withstand the rough weather of life, the ups and downs of our own experience. The Lord used this metaphor to explain His saving mission: "The rain descended, and the floods came, and the winds blew, and beat upon that house; and it fell not: for it was founded upon a rock."[2]

The hymn continues by telling of the security that comes from opening our hearts and minds to the Lord's protective power. The Rock is cleft—that is, separated or divided—to create a space within, where we can find refuge in the encircling warmth of His saving embrace. This comforting image of being surrounded by an accepting fortress of stone tells of the real safety that comes from righteous living. The Lord has unconditional love for all people. He is open to us, even when our hearts have been as hard as stone. We need only open ourselves to His redeeming love, have a humble heart and a contrite spirit, and He will receive us.

"Let me hide myself in thee." This very personal plea for refuge highlights the intimacy of our salvation and the promise of His peace. The Lord's invitation is both universal and individual. He beckons, "Come unto me, all ye that labour and are heavy laden, and I will give you rest."[3] While He invites *all* who labor, each of us must personally respond. We must find our way to Him, and to His comfort and rest. The last verse of this hymn tells of that rest and reminds us of His lasting peace:

> While I draw this fleeting breath,
> When mine eyes shall close in death,
> When I rise to worlds unknown
> And behold thee on thy throne,
> Rock of Ages, cleft for me,
> Let me hide myself in thee.

1. In *Hymns of The Church of Jesus Christ of Latter-day Saints* (Salt Lake City: The Church of Jesus Christ of Latter-day Saints, 1985), no. 111.
2. Matthew 7:25.
3. Matthew 11:28.

At One

Our hearts and minds turn to that night two thousand years ago with yearning. Oh, that we might have been there, too, and seen the baby, held Him, fallen to our knees with joy that at last God was with us.

What did Mary know as she held her infant close? Certainly enough that she couldn't say, only pondered it in her heart as she had done for months. One writer tried to imagine her feelings: "Oh, let me enfold Thee, my baby tonight, while legions are singing in joyous delight. A new star has risen to hail Thee divine, For you are a King, but tonight you are mine."[1]

Did Mary cast her mind ahead to Gethsemane or Golgotha as she held her baby? A mother and her newborn infant are almost one. He recognizes her heartbeat as the most comforting sound he knows. She stares at him with wonder, memorizing each movement, each yawn and stretch, so they will ever be with her. The protection she has given him for months, as he has grown, extends beyond birth. Not pain, not rejection for this precious child, she must have thought. Not His flesh torn, not the agony of the sins of the world for Him.

But the oneness of a mother and child, the complete identification between them, is only the reminder of another kind of oneness—being at one with God. It is that greater oneness that Christ came to provide.

His atonement was not just for our sins but for all the grief, carelessness, and inadequacy we experience as mortals on this earth. It was for all the range of anguish and bitterness that comes into our lives—those things that bring discord, destroy our peace, and break our hearts. Those things that divide us from God. Jesus Christ came to make us at one again by paying our debts and taking our burdens upon Him—debts too big to pay ourselves, burdens too heavy to carry.

As He said during His ministry, "The Spirit of the Lord is upon me, because he hath anointed me to preach the gospel to the poor; he hath sent me to heal the brokenhearted, to preach deliverance to the captives, . . . to set at liberty them that are bruised."[2] It is through our Savior that we are healed.

The mother who held her child close at Bethlehem stood at His cross only a few years later. The child who had once been hers had atoned for all of us.

....

1. Bertha A. Kleinman, "Mary's Lullaby," Wanda West Palmer Publishing.
2. Luke 4:18.

A Celebration of Life

A BIRTHDAY PARTY on the grandest scale, Christmas is a celebration of life—new life, eternal life, even "the way, the truth, and the life."[1] To feel the spirit of Christmas is to drink from the well of living water.

Consider the birth of a child. Have you noticed how a baby—the fragile embodiment of new life—enlivens its parents, siblings, grandparents, and all who share in its birth? New mothers, who have felt life quicken and grow within them, radiate a heavenly love. New fathers walk with a spirited and knowing step, for sleeping in a cradle is a child they love. Siblings experience newfound wonder, even awe, for they have witnessed the miracle of birth. Grandparents' eyes are filled with a sparkle—maybe even overflowing with tears—for in each new grandchild they sense the abundance of never-ending life. Such is the power of a single birth—any birth.

Consider, then, the birth of the Son of God. Certainly Mary, God's handmaiden, radiated heavenly light. No doubt Joseph walked with great anticipation and understanding. Friends, siblings, and even grandparents were not present to share in this sacred event in a quiet stable. And yet, each of them—every man and woman ever born—could partake of the new life He brought. In the grown Child's own words, "I am come that they might have life, and that they might have it more abundantly."[2]

Perhaps that is what Christmas is all about: learning to "have life" and to "have it more abundantly." If any word could characterize this season of celebration, it would be *lively*. The giving and receiving, the eager anticipation, the traditions and decorations all seem to bring new life—even more abundant living—to those who participate. Children dance with glee, parents bustle with excitement, neighbors and friends are full of good cheer, families gather for fun and festivities.

It's all part of the grand and glorious birthday celebration that began a long time ago in Bethlehem, when angels sang, gifts were given, and a bright star shone in the heavens. Each carol, every sparkling light, and all the Christmas trees pointing heavenward recall the majesty of that birth—and, with them, the promise of a more abundant life.

The words of a familiar carol proclaim that He was "born that man no more may die; born to raise the sons of earth, born to give them second birth. Hark! the herald angels sing glory to the newborn king."[3] May His birth and life enrich ours each Christmas season—and throughout the year.

1. John 14:6.
2. John 10:10.
3. Charles Wesley, "Hark! the Herald Angels Sing," *Hymns of The Church of Jesus Christ of Latter-day Saints* (Salt Lake City: The Church of Jesus Christ of Latter-day Saints, 1985), no. 209.

Not for Want of a Star

As LONG AS LANGUAGE SURVIVES, the story of the three wise men who followed the star to Bethlehem will be told. And, regardless of the myths that have grown up and around the meager account, the narrative is of timeless value, for it represents, in a very real way, the long history of man's search for truth—the doubt, the risk, the effort, the cost.

If experience is any teacher, the Magi were not called wise by their peers, for followers of distant stars have never been called wise. No doubt they were called foolish—foolish for leaving their homes and families in search of a dream, foolish for not requiring more specific proof to support their belief, foolish for giving up career and status, foolish for caring about truth at all.

But these were no ordinary men. They had not forgotten that the untiring pursuit of a faraway truth is what alone gives meaning and substance to life. Discovery, challenge, investigation in search of the dim horizon—this was the quest of the wise men.

So, on they trudged across valley and over mountain pass, through burning days and freezing nights, pushing and pulling their sore-footed camels.

And then, following their laborious journey, they returned to their houses and families, broken and poor, but richer by far than those who had stayed at home—for their hope had turned to faith.

Thus, the nameless Magi take their place alongside the other heroes of history: with takers of untraveled roads, sailors of deep waters, riders of whirlwinds, dreamers of dreams.

Twenty wide centuries have come and gone since then; time has done its best to tarnish the star's luster. The imagination and childlike wonder of the Magi have been replaced by the cold mistrust of an age that values body over spirit, convenience over sacrifice. The star that led the wise men is no longer visible against the darkened firmament.

But it may be that our own skepticism, our materialism, our disregard for truth itself have dimmed the star's splendor.

Perhaps, with a brilliance the cynical vision of modern man cannot divine, the star that led the Magi to the Holy Child of Bethlehem still shines, illuminating the darkness for those who have eyes to see.

And, if today there are none to make the difficult journey to where Truth lies hidden in swaddling clothes—it may not be because there is no star but because there are no wise men.

Anticipating Christmas

CHRISTMAS IS COMING.

For almost twenty centuries, that message has brought hope and anticipation. While Christmas hearkens back to that holy night in Bethlehem, the glory of the holiday is also in its focus on the future—in the excitement of good things to come.

We anticipate and prepare for this holiday like no other. The shopping, the wrapping, the decorating—these all add to the spirit of the occasion. Many children have little calendars with doors to open for every approaching day—or paper chains from which they detach a link each day—to mark the coming of Christmas. The gaily wrapped presents prompt the imagination. The festive aromas tantalize the taste buds.

Certainly, hope and anticipation are appropriate attitudes at Christmastime. The first Christmas was the fulfillment of centuries of hope. Prophets had foretold that a Messiah would come to save His people. The believers waited and watched for the signs. Even in far-off lands of the East, wise men were aware that certain changes in the heavens would mark the coming of the King of the Jews. Hope and anticipation led them to follow a star to Bethlehem.

The scholars of Herod's court were likewise acquainted with the scriptural promises. They were quick to inform the king that the Messiah would be born in Bethlehem as the prophets had predicted.

As it was on that first Christmas day, so it is today. The great appeal of anticipation brings us back to the baby in Bethlehem. Many hopes were realized with the coming of the Christ child. But much was foretold that night that has not yet been fulfilled. The angels promised peace on earth and goodwill toward all men. Scanning yesterday's history or today's headlines quickly tells us how far we are from that heavenly state.

The beautiful scene of a child loved and cared for gives us hope that one day all children will be welcomed—with anticipation. The innocent baby Jesus helps us look to the day when each of us all over the world will be sinless once again.

The summation of all these symbols is our promise of a better world. Each Christmas brings us closer to that blessed day. Again the anticipation rises each year. The hope of that holy night again sustains us. Be of good cheer, for Christmas is coming.

Each New Christmas,
the Same Hope of Christ

THE CELEBRATION OF CHRISTMAS is nearly two thousand years old. We look forward to all the happy decoration and ritual by which we remember the birth of Christ. From many cultures have come emblems and symbols that remind us of the age-old promise of Christ's coming—of His birth and mission. All over the world, we burn yule logs or decorate Christmas trees or hang stockings and mistletoe. We sing carols and bake Christmas treats to make special this time when we remember His birth.

But, although Christmas is comfortable and familiar to most of us, the Christmas season is "new" to many this year. Many children are for the first time discovering the wonder of anticipating gifts. Many adults this year will newly learn the spirit of giving and receiving and, for the first time, feel the deep gratitude of this season. And, for many who have despaired because of the duplicities and disappointments of this world, Christmas this season provides a "new" opportunity to take hope in the gifts of Jesus.

A philosopher recently asked a disturbing question about the hope we have in Christ. The philosopher reasoned that, if we can be so mistaken about one another, how can we be so sure of Him who we have not seen—whose audible voice we may not have heard—from whom so many of us have been so far removed?

The first part of the question is undeniable. We are frequently mistaken about one another. We do the best we can to love and be loved; but, in the end, we may find it difficult to answer even for ourselves, much less for someone else. We may be unrequited in our affections, disappointed in our love. We may have confidence in persons who earn our trust only to betray it. Family and friends are all free to choose and, in their choosing, may choose against us.

But such disappointments and betrayals are bound by time; they may be terrible in the moment, but they are the momentary pains of this world. And, even in this world, they may be reversed. Those who have ceased to love us may yet love us again. The wounds we bear may be bandaged and healed.

How different for us is the hope of Jesus, which is not bound by time nor tempered by earthly circumstances of another's choice. Beyond the help and hope we have in this world of beginnings and endings is the hope of Him who was born in Bethlehem, who promises to restore all our losses and heal all our hurts, who will sustain us and be our friend when time itself has passed away.

How can we trust in Him? *How can we not?* The familiar spirit of Christmas is made new in each of us as we recognize our need for Jesus—as we accept our hope in Christ. For, while all the world is changing—while *even we* are changeable—He is the same, our hope in Him is the same, the promise of His birth is the same . . . *forever.*

PART 4

Peace and the Power of Love

The Power of Love

Love's POWER TO TRANSFORM, to see the princess in the ordinary girl, to rescue the prince from his beastly form is a "tale as old as time, [a] song as old as rhyme."[1] We all know the story, for, at some point, perhaps we've all been beauties and loved apparent beasts, seeing beyond surfaces and loving deeper than looks. And we've all probably had beastly moments, too, disguising our real needs with the trappings of independence and barring out pain and rejection by refusing to care—or to be cared for.

At such moments, perhaps we have witnessed the power of love. Just when we thought love would pass us by—just when we thought ourselves unlovable, maybe even when we felt undeserving of affection—some beautiful person reached out with a blind but all-seeing love.

Such was the case with Rostand's Cyrano de Bergerac—a gifted poet, a powerful swordsman, a loyal friend, and yet a most unpleasant face—who, with his protruding nose, thought himself so ugly, so unlovable, that he wouldn't declare his love to the beautiful Roxane until it was too late. On his deathbed, Cyrano revealed his true feelings for her, still disbelieving that his love could ever be returned. But, to his surprise, Roxane proclaimed her undying love for him. Cyrano lamented the unbelievable reality of it all: "When Beauty said, 'I love you' to the Beast that was a fairy prince, his ugliness changed and dissolved, like magic. . . . But you see I am still the same."[2]

For Roxane, however, his ugliness had "changed and dis-

117

solved" a long time ago. If only he would have let this beauty into his life earlier. If only he would have forgotten his beastly face, perhaps he would have realized that—like Roxane—there were those who could see past his ugly nose and love him for the noble man he was. His life would have been different, his love so much more full.

Not only do we have the opportunity to love those who think themselves unlovable, but we also have the responsibility to let others love us. No matter who we are, no matter how we look, no matter how life may have changed us, we all need love. And we can all give love. Regardless of the beastly layers we may hide beneath, we must let the beauty back in. For, as Shakespeare has written:

> Love is not love
> Which alters when it alteration finds,
>
> . . . .
>
> O, no! It is an ever-fixèd mark,
> That looks on tempests and is never shaken.

---

1. Howard Ashman and Alan Menken, "Beauty and the Beast" (Walt Disney Music Company and Wonderland Music Company, 1991).
2. Edmond Rostand, *Cyrano de Bergerac* (New York: Random House, 1951), p. 295.
3. Sonnet 116, in Angela Partington, ed., *The Oxford Dictionary of Quotations* (New York: Oxford, 1992), p. 634.

Love Is Eternal

ABRAHAM LINCOLN is known for many wise sayings, but one of his most meaningful mottos was a secret. For a time, only his wife was privy to the wisdom Lincoln had engraved on the inside of her wedding ring: "Love is eternal." These appropriate, even prophetic words saw the Lincolns through many trying moments. When burdened by financial failure, civil war, public discord, family strife, and prolonged illness, Mr. and Mrs. Lincoln held true to the belief that love transcends all. One historian noted that their marriage was a triumph of love over the odds, surviving everything—including death.[1]

This idea that love can be forever enriches our lives and deepens our understanding. When we realize that feelings of the heart span more than a lifetime, simple courtesies, kind gestures, and all demonstrations of love take on more significance. Time spent with children, visits to grandparents' homes, quiet moments with our spouses, and heart-to-heart conversations with loved ones are investments with eternal returns.

Certainly, the feelings of love that we cultivate here will not be lost to eternity. David O. McKay explained: "Love is the most divine attribute of the human soul, and if you accept the immortality of the soul, that is, if you believe that personality persists after death, then, you must believe that love also lives."[2] Death's door could not be so final to close off real affection. When we have laughed and cried with someone, taught and been taught, given and taken, forgiven and been forgiven—in other words, when we have loved and been loved—we cannot help but know that love is everlasting.

Just like the ring upon which Lincoln engraved "Love is eternal," the love of God is eternal, without beginning or end, an all-encompassing circle. Thousands of years ago, the Lord told Jeremiah, "I have loved thee with an everlasting love."[3] And His words are just as true today. As God so completely and eternally loves, may we love, engraving in our minds and on our hearts the words "Love is Eternal."

1. Justin G. Turner and Linda Turner, *Mary Todd Lincoln, Her Life and Letters* (New York: Fromm International Publishing Corporation, 1987), p. 30.

2. *Gospel Ideals: Selections from the Discourses of David O. McKay* (Salt Lake City: Improvement Era, 1953), p. 463.

3. Jeremiah 31:3.

Loving Our Neighbor

Most of us believe we should love humanity, that we are a community of brothers and sisters on this earth linked in more ways than we know. We look at pictures of suffering children in faraway lands and our hearts are torn with sorrow. We grieve when we read in the newspaper of tragic accidents.

But it is interesting that sometimes it is easier to love people in general than people in particular, easier to love humanity than a particular neighbor whose habits irritate us. That is probably because we never associate with all of humanity. We can believe we are a caring person without any nagging evidence to the contrary when it comes to loving everyone. "Do I love my neighbor? Yes, I do," most of us can answer when we think of people in general. Humanity in general never puts us to the test to see if our ideals really stick.

However, people in particular often put our ideals to the test: a particular child may defy us, disappoint us, or scream out in anger; a particular colleague at work wants the same assignment or promotion we do; a particular driver on the road honks at us; a particular friend judges us wrongly; a particular workman doesn't do the job we've paid him to do. Humanity in general is easy to love. It is people in particular we have difficulty with.

Yet, in this marvelous school called life, how we respond to people in particular is the true test of character. If the Lord has asked us to love another, we cannot make exceptions, saying, "I can love everyone but him" or "I can love everyone but her." The

Lord makes no exceptions when he asks us to love one another. He makes no qualifications. It is not to love until we are crossed, or love until we are irritated, or love until our feelings are hurt. It is not to love until someone wears out our love and it runs dry.

We each must search our hearts to see if we harbor ill will toward others. Where there is enmity we must not allow ourselves any justification or excuse. Enmity is not from the Lord. It is a darkness that can grow to swamp all our good feelings.

We must ask ourselves the hard questions: "Do I see myself in a continual contest with others where only one can win? Do I feel a need to be more important than others? Am I slow to forgive and do I hold onto grudges? Do I always feel the need to be right? It is difficult to have any of these feelings at the same time we truly love our neighbor as ourselves.

We have not been asked to love people in general. We have been asked to love each person, one at a time with all the attending imperfections and shortcomings. It is with that powerful, personal approach that the Lord loves us.

Loving Our Neighbor
in a Shrinking World

OUR WORLD seems to get smaller every day. Travel and commu-
nications are shrinking the distances between us. Multinational
business are bridging boundaries, and ecological systems are inter-
twining and affecting one another.

As people are drawn closer together, we have a greater and
greater effect on each other. John Donne wrote three and a half
centuries ago, "No man is an island. . . ; every man is a piece of the
continent."[1]

We are neighbors on this steadily shrinking continent called
earth, and we will all be happier as we learn to care for and co-
operate with each other. Jesus said we should love our neighbor as
ourselves. We may think that loving ourselves is easy. But, in fact,
most disrespect for others springs from a lack of self-respect.
When we feel inadequate and unworthy, we may downgrade others to try to make ourselves look better. Families, cultures, and
nations can fall into this unloving relationship. History is filled
with border disputes, feuds, war, and bloodshed arising from self-
hatred transferred to our neighbors.

Each of us is a child of God. We are worthy and capable of
receiving and giving love. As we accept this fact and humbly love
ourselves, we are freed of the need to denigrate others.

Our next step on the road to loving others will probably be
to love those who are like us. It is relatively easy to love people

who share our opinions, lifestyles, and tastes. There is nothing wrong with loving those who are similar to us, but restricting our love to only this inner circle is very confining. We exclude the vast majority of the human race who are different from ourselves.

The next phase, then, is to learn to love others despite our differences. When we reach this point, we may feel we have arrived, but there is one more step in this journey. That is when we love others, not in spite of their differences but because of their differences. We do not ask or expect that others change to become more lovable to us. We love them as they are. This ultimate view of human relationships was described by Jesus when He said, "Love your enemies, bless them that curse you, do good to them that hate you, and pray for them which despitefully use you, and persecute you."[2]

To reach out to those who differ from us, despise us, hate and harm us—this is the mark of true maturity as a human being. It is not easy. But it can be done. Someone must break the cycle of mutual recrimination that exists when we love only our own and hate those outside our circle.

Let us pray to God to give us courage to reach beyond our comfortable associates; wisdom to understand and appreciate the good in every person; and the strength to love even those who hate us. As we do, the binding together that is coming with our shrinking world will become, in fact, a bonding of human hearts into a better world.

1. In John Bartlett, *Familiar Quotations,* edited by Emily Morison Beck (Boston: Little, Brown and Co., 1980), p. 254.
2. Matthew 5:44.

The Joy of Married Love

....

THE WORLD IS FULL OF LOVE STORIES. He and she—apart in the world—always feel somehow incomplete. They search, not always knowing what they search for, until they find each other. In marriage, the two become one. He is the completion of her soul.

Scholar Joseph Campbell saw this pattern in the myths he studied from cultures across the earth. "Myth," he found, "helps you to put your mind in touch with this experience of being alive."[1] And, in myth, he found what marriage is: "Originally you were one. You are now two in the world, but the recognition of the spiritual identity is what marriage is."[2]

Those who have been happily married rejoice in the depth of that spiritual identity they share. One man, who lived in the nineteenth century, wrote this prayer for his wife: "Oh God . . . wilt Thou bless her with peace and with a long life; and when Thou shalt see fit to take her, let [me] go with her; and dwell with each other throughout eternity; that no power shall ever separate us from each other; for Thou . . . knowest we love each other with pure hearts. . . . Now, . . . hear Thy servant, and let us have the desires of our hearts; for we want to live together, and die, and be buried, and rise and reign together in Thy kingdom with our dear children."[3]

When we hear this depth of feeling, we almost wonder if such emotion is possible in our world today. All around us we see examples of love that is fleeting—commitment that it temporary. We see emotions that are stirred and then die again, vanished like

125

yesterday's style. Perhaps it is because we have forgotten what marriage is. We become distracted by the first flurries of romantic attachment—and call that love. We find someone physically attractive—and call that love.

The love that becomes a joyful marriage is spiritual identity. It says, "If it matters to you, then it matters to me." It says, "I can count on you under all circumstances." It says, "I am safe in your love. When I stumble on my weaknesses, you are not critical. I am a soul in the process of unfolding, and you accept me where I am. Because you love me, I am free to grow."

Is this kind of love really possible today? Yes, it is. But we must remember that it is the Lord who makes it possible. "Beloved," said John, "let us love one another: for love is of God; and every one that loveth is born of God, and knoweth God."[4] The kind of love that transforms two into one is a gift from God; and, if we want it enough, He is the one who can show us the way. We have to be willing to be transformed by Him into people far more capable of love than we are. We have to learn the fine lessons of forgiveness, patience, courage in the face of trial, vision. As our hearts are changed through His love, we can, in turn, learn to love. Then, and only then, can we put our days of loneliness behind us to move into days of joy.

1. Joseph Campbell with Bill Moyers, *The Power of Myth*, edited by Betty Sue Flowers (New York: Doubleday, 1988), p. 6.
2. Ibid.
3. Orson F. Whitney, *Life of Heber C. Kimball* (Salt Lake City: Bookcraft, 1945), p. 335.
4. 1 John 4:7.

The Unrighteousness of Rage

As Christians, we are taught by the scriptures that our lives should be directed by love; love unfeigned; love so encompassing and complete that it subsumes all lesser emotions and calms us with its sweet instruction.

We do love. We love family and friends. We love pets, projects, people, places, food, and football. But is this loving, the love of which the scriptures speak? Does it dedicate and define our lives?

One of the paradoxes of our loving is that many of the people we most love are most likely to make us angry. Our children frustrate our dreams for them and disappoint our designs for their future. Our spouses may be so closely linked with our living that the ways in which they are different from us inconvenience and aggravate us. We may find ourselves actually being more angry than loving in our associations with those for whom we most proclaim our love.

Partly, this is because we place so much importance in these relationships—because we value them. We may be fearful for them, and the regressions of fear can quickly spark the emotional gap and be turned into angry aggression. We should not take comfort nor find excuse in such explanations of our anger. Anger kills love, and there is no righteousness in our common rages.

Some may point to the infrequent anger of the Savior and find expiation for their sins of rage. Such allusions are weak arguments. The Lord has told us: "I will forgive whom I will forgive;

but unto you it is given to forgive all men." The Lord's motives are pure; ours are not. The Lord is not corrupted by His emotions and His responses; we are. For this reason, He has commanded us to love one another, to take love as our instruction and our motivation.

This commandment is not easy. Even those we love, perhaps especially those we love, may try our patience and tempt us to surrender the gentle genius of love. When we surrender to the temptations of anger, we almost always surrender our ability to love. We may try to tell ourselves otherwise. We may attempt to argue that our indignation is righteous, that our anger is not aggressive but protective, that our rage is redemptive. But they are not. If we practice love, and believe in love, and give ourselves to love, we will be more loving, less angry—and our world and the world of those we love will be a better place.

Do Good, Seek Peace

In these turbulent times of change and confusion, we pause to ponder peace. In all times and places, nothing has been more valued, no goal more worthy. Since the beginning, men and women have desired peace for their hearts, homes, communities, and countries. And yet, all the while there are those who thrive on chaos—those who seek noise and shun the sounds of silence.

While we may sincerely hope and even strive for a peaceful world, we must first find peace in our hearts. For, without this, nothing else matters. As Neal A. Maxwell has questioned: "Can there, in fact, be peace in the world if there is not peace in our homes as well as in our hearts? Can we, in fact, really expect to have peace in the world if the civil wars raging inside so many individuals do not subside?"[1]

These "raging civil wars" inside us may be born of selfishness, insecurity, even jealousy and envy. We may live in financial prosperity and yet be spiritually impoverished. Or, in poverty, we may sense the need for something more than money. At the center of our hearts, in our very souls, we may feel hollow—like something essential is missing. And what's often missing is the peace of righteous living.

Real peace comes from God. We know from divine directive that "God is not the author of confusion but of peace."[2] And the Apostle Paul counseled that we "live in peace; and the God of love and peace shall be with you."[3] But how can we feel peaceful when unrest comes in daily doses, and noise is a national habit?

Peace requires deep faith in God and in life. Peace takes patience and practice, effort and energy. And peace comes from humbly doing our best, following God's commands, and helping others. For, as the psalmist has said, "Do good; seek peace."[4] These simple phrases that bring comfort to our souls, in practice, are inseparable. When we do good, we find peace. Or we seek and find peace by doing good. Let us spread peace throughout the world—one heart at a time—by seeking for peace within ourselves and by giving goodness to others.

1. *Sermons Not Spoken* (Salt Lake City: Bookcraft, 1985), p. 36.
2. 1 Corinthians 14:33.
3. 2 Corinthians 13:11.
4. Psalm 34:14.

In Hope of Peace

....

$\mathbb{P}$EACE AND FREEDOM are not merely desirable; they are the God-given rights of all people. As the psalmist declared, "The Lord will give strength unto his people; the Lord will bless his people with peace."[1]

His words were prophetic to the fact that our world is full of trouble. In one moment whole nations find their way into the light of self-determination; and in the next moment tyrants assault and attempt to take that freedom away. We live in a world in which even the "men of peace" frequently cannot find peace.

Thus the study of war has become a fundamental education for governments and societies. Wars of aggression. Wars of oppression. Wars of correction and self-protection. Whatever the cause, however just the purpose, one of the results of war is always the same: men and women are called upon to defend these God-given rights of peace and freedom.

The nineteenth-century British poet Rudyard Kipling, himself no stranger to the many military crusades of his own country and time, looked upon the adventuring of war and was afraid. The triumphs of battle can be so seductive as to make us forget that our God is a God of peace.

"Still stands thine ancient sacrifice," Kipling wrote, and he prayed: "Lord God of Hosts, be with us yet, lest we forget."[2] Lest we forget that there is no peace in war, only hope for peace. The vision of God's prophets and the hope of his people have always been to see beyond war, to anticipate the times of peace and that final Time of Peace. As the prophet Isaiah wrote, "They shall beat their swords into plowshares and their spears into pruning hooks; nation shall not lift up sword against nation, neither shall they learn war any more."[3]

This vision of a world in which war is no longer a solution does not diminish our love nor our hope for those on both sides afflicted by the cruel demands of war. We have feelings of pride and appreciation for those men and women who, during these difficult times, are serving and sacrificing in the armed forces of our country. Both the soldier and the civilian are war's victims, and we pray for them all. We pray that the power of tyrants may be set aside. We pray that the price of peace may ultimately be paid with a coin not minted in the blood of our loved ones. We pray that even as we give honor and pay homage to the many acts of courage, heroism, and sacrifice that spring out of war, we will not forget that one of the prices of peace is not victory but surrender: the surrendering of ourselves to the "peace of God, which passeth all understanding,"[4] the surrendering of *our* lives to *His* way of life. And finally, the surrendering of war.

We may not live in such a world yet. But each of us must become part of the struggle to help usher in that world of peace.

1. Psalm 29:11.
2. "God of Our Fathers, Known of Old," *Hymns of The Church of Jesus Christ of Latter-day Saints* (Salt Lake City: The Church of Jesus Christ of Latter-day Saints, 1985), no. 80.
3. Isaiah 2:4.
4. Philippians 4:7.

Jerusalem Has a Heart

JERUSALEM, CITY OF LIGHT, has a heart. And in it is the story of the human family.

Jerusalem is the reality and the symbol of the heights of civilization and sanctity; yet, it has often been ravaged by degradation. It is a birthplace and a death place of the highest in man. To this hour, the city is an unspeakably powerful lure to the religious impulses of the peacemaker. But few cities have witnessed as much of war and laying waste. It reminds us that there is no invincible city in the world—that violence may erupt anywhere, anytime.

Today, as we walk the streets, we see in the eyes of little children innocence gone, inner light dimmed, hope and high purpose overshadowed by the stirrings of bitterness. Are those of us who call ourselves mature blind to the wounds in these eyes and in the eyes of such children throughout the world? Or seeing, do we care? Or caring, do we care enough to change our own ways of relating? Can we learn to think with our hearts?

One morning last year, Jerusalem awoke to deep snow. Nothing like it had occurred in a hundred years. Suddenly, adults became children and children became themselves—filled with wonder. Enmities faded, scorn was forgotten, a new set of energies emerged. People poured out of their homes, and in their meetings and partings, in work and in travel, they threw handfuls of snow as they would throw kisses. They laughed, rolled, embraced, jumped in a swirl of goodwill. Every human contact was humane.

133

Celebration, sharing, and a tangible peace filled the air. Then, the snow melted and ancient tensions and conflicts resumed.

The experience proved one thing: in the most closed center self may rest the capacity to be open, joyful, humane. In the stoniest of hearts, there is potential for softening. In the most strained of relationships, there is possible renewal of kinship. When we choose to see ourselves and others with new eyes, new life may come into us.

Jerusalem teaches that the pulse that throbs with life and love, rather than with vengeance, is true. Jerusalem sings to us that the childlike, and holy, impulse to peace is real maturity. Jerusalem pleads with us that, when this divine impulse is followed, God will awaken us to the new morning and the new beginning that will be the end of the war in human hearts. Then, even while civilizations crumble, civilization will flourish.

The Spirit of Giving

THEY SAW THE YOUNG CHILD with Mary his mother, and fell down, and worshipped him: and when they had opened their treasures, they presented unto him gifts; gold, and frankincense, and myrrh."[1] In the true spirit of giving, these wise men shared their treasures with the infant King. Certainly, such wise men would know that the child had little use for fine fragrances and precious metals. But, for them, the treasures were symbols of their search, of their willingness to give all to know Him.

And from their heartfelt giving emerges a tradition of sharing that is so much a part of us. During this Christmas season, do we—like the wise men of old—"fall down and worship him" by giving of our time, treasures, thoughts, and feelings?

In many ways, our manner of giving tells of our convictions, priorities, and devotions. When we give of our time, on a regular and responsible basis, we clearly show that we care. When we give of our substance—unselfishly—we build bridges of love. When we risk sharing our real feelings, we develop relationships of understanding and trust. For we cannot really care or be cared for, love or be loved, understand or be understood, unless we are willing to open our treasures of time, substances, and self.

Such wholehearted giving is not easily accomplished. It requires humility and effort, tireless energy, and sometimes even courage. But, as Paul taught, "It is more blessed to give than to receive."[2] And the Lord Himself gave us some guidelines for giving when He instructed His disciples: "Give to him that asketh

135

thee, and from him that would borrow of thee turn not thou away"[3] and "Freely ye have received, freely give."[4]

Cultivate a spirit of such generous giving by leaving that comfort zone where we may thoughtlessly abide and mechanically give. Really search for stars under which you can open your treasures. For the wise man or woman is still he or she who seeks for the King of kings and finds Him through selflessly giving—not just at Christmas, the season of giving, but all year, and in all ways. By so sharing, we come to know the Giver of all good gifts, the Son of God, even Christ our Lord.

1. Matthew 2:11.
2. Acts 20:35.
3. Matthew 5:42.
4. Matthew 10:8.

Free Gifts

THE BEST GIFTS are those that are freely given. Without obligation, duty, or the expectation of getting something in return, free gifts can be true expressions of love. They frequently come from the familiar but unknown donor we call "anonymous." But they also come from the hearts and homes of those we know best. And sometimes, such free gifts are so generously given that we don't even realize we've received them.

They are usually wrapped in service and always decorated with love. Gifts, freely given, may take the form of kindness, respect, and loyalty. Or they may come in the more tangible form of food and shelter. In any case, the gift is without price or the promise of requital. Because the giver of such gifts knows that freely giving is its own reward, he or she doesn't hang the gift over the receiver's head—or heart.

One young father opened a storehouse of free gifts upon becoming a parent himself. He realized how generously his own parents had given of their time, energy, and love upon caring for a child of his own: the busy days, the sleepless nights, the tears, and the smiles. And yet, he was never made to feel indebted through the years. Perhaps that's why his gratitude was so full now. The very parents who had given a portion of their lives to him encouraged him to have a life of his own. They had freely given of their love. And, because of that, the love their adult son now gave them was also a free gift. Perhaps the best kind.

Anne Morrow Lindbergh explains this kind of priceless

exchange in terms of her experience with the sea. She receives great treasures of knowledge from the age-old teacher—free gifts of insight and understanding. And yet, "the sea does not reward those who are too anxious, too greedy, or too impatient. To dig for treasures shows not only impatience and greed, but lack of faith,"[1] she says. Only as she sits on the beach and opens herself up to its beauty, does it reveal itself. Only then do the shells surface; only then do the snails curl up beside her. In others words, we cannot force, demand, or require gifts from the sea, but they are freely given to us as we patiently—and without expectation—spend time on the shore.

Free gifts, whether they come from the sea, our parents, or any generous donor, can inspire real feelings of gratitude and active desires to return favors. Because we are all freely loved by God, we can each feel to "sing the song of redeeming love."[2] In His own powerful words, "freely ye have received, freely give."[3]

1. Anne Morrow Lindbergh, *Gift from the Sea* (New York: Vintage, 1978), p. 17.
2. Alma 5:26.
3. Matthew 10:8.

Freedom to Choose

During the season of patriotic celebration, we remember our sacred freedoms. Well over two hundred years ago, courageous colonists adopted a Declaration of Independence, announced their separation from Great Britain, and created the United States of America. We honor their sacrifice; we thank them for their fight. But could we better describe their revolution as a restoration?

Certainly, from a historical perspective, these patriots were revolting against tyranny. But, perhaps from God's eternal perspective, they were restoring a universal birthright: the freedom to choose. Alexander Hamilton, a freedom fighter himself, wrote: "The Sacred Rights of Mankind are not to be rummaged for among old parchments or musty records. They are written, as with a sunbeam, in the whole volume of human nature, by the Hand of Divinity . . . , and can never be erased or obscured by mortal power."[1]

Prophets made such pronouncements long ago. Joshua's words of wisdom might well have been the colonists' battle cry: "Choose you this day whom ye will serve."[2] They fought to choose; they died to be free.

Their purpose was to create a new home, a new life, even a new way of thinking, that they might uphold the privilege of choosing. The struggle for freedom was long and painful. Farmers became soldiers, mothers became martyrs, lawyers became statesmen, and citizens became philosophers to reclaim this basic birthright. Their battles were declarations of faith, of principle, of belief.

Those same desires for freedom inspire us today. The eternal and universal right to be free is reaffirmed all over the world. Nations are struggling with newly won liberties. Governments are adjusting to more openness and opportunity. Individuals are flexing their newly freed muscles. There are growing pains and problems, to be sure. But small seeds of freedom will continue to grow and flourish as long as people live and breathe—as long as people trust in God.

This, then, is the real heritage of the American colonists: a restoration of our God-given agency—that we, like the Israelites of old, might choose this day whom we will serve. Let us respect the faithful fight of our forefathers by not abusing this hard-won trust. And, to our God who gave us this liberty, we gratefully sing, "Lord God of Hosts, be with us yet, lest we forget, lest we forget."[3]

1. Clinton Rossiter, *The Political Thought of the American Revolution* (Harcourt, Brace & World, 1963), p. 107.
2. Joshua 24:15.
3. "God of Our Fathers, Known of Old," *Hymns of The Church of Jesus Christ of Latter-day Saints* (Salt Lake City: The Church of Jesus Christ of Latter-day Saints, 1985), no. 80.

True Heroes

FROM THE BEGINNING of time, humanity has worshipped heroes: King Arthur, Hercules, Beowulf. Hundreds of years have passed since these names were first spoken, and they still evoke feelings of veneration.

Our twentieth century has its own heroes; we love to talk about them, yearn to learn more of them, try to imitate them. We reward our heroes with fortunes, with praise, and with power.

Wouldn't it be interesting, however, if God were to show us a few whom He considered heroes? How would they compare to the worldly heroes we honor? If He were to name them, whom would He choose?

Machiavelli believed that we honor those who get ahead in three areas: money, fame, and power. Would God—the creator of every jewel, every vein of gold—be impressed by worldly riches? Would He who guides the destiny of nations be awed by those who capture headlines? Would He who poured energy into suns and set galaxies hurtling through space be impressed by worldly power?

The truth is, even though God may appreciate the physical strength of a man who can lift his weight in iron, He appreciates far more the inner strength of a man who can lift another's spirit. And, while the heavenly hosts may admire the woman who can build an edifice that towers into the clouds, they admire more the woman who can build within her a towering faith.

God's heroes are conspicuous for their humility, preferring

that their good deeds go undiscovered; they are concerned more for others' needs than for their own. They are not consumed with things nor driven to acquire riches but, instead, freely give of their time, of their skills, of their substance.

The names of the world's heroes are written on the pages of the newspapers; the names of God's heroes are written on the hearts of the hungry, the hurt, the unhappy.

They rarely make the evening news, rarely leave behind great wealth; statues are rarely molded in their likeness. But they always leave behind a legacy of humble service that speaks more eloquently than any monument or myth ever could. These are they who love God with all their heart; these are they who love their fellow man. These are they who give us a glimpse of what it means to be a true hero.

The Power of Praise

....

THE HIGHLY DECORATED STATESMAN, the Duke of Wellington, was asked late in life what he would have done differently. He did not say he would change the way he fought the magnificent Battle of Waterloo—or any other battle. He simply said, "I should have given more praise."[1]

We all have the need to be accepted and appreciated. Because we're all trying, we need to know that our daily efforts to change and improve are acknowledged by someone. We all need to know that we matter.

Unfortunately, some of us go through the day never hearing a kind word, an encouraging comment, or even the faintest expression of praise. And yet, it only takes seconds of time and ounces of energy to let others know that we appreciate them. It takes so little effort to offer a simple word of encouragement, to acknowledge genuine growth and real effort.

Sincere praise can be a sustaining force for us throughout our lives. Words of praise and feelings of commendation are never forgotten. How many of us remember kind words that were spoken to us years ago? How many of us still hold on to a compliment we received as a child?

With those expressions of encouragement, we build reservoirs of praise that we—as well as our children, spouses, and friends—can continue to draw upon. Those daily deposits of praise and approval both strengthen the sender and encourage the receiver. They motivate us to give more praise, and they inspire us to live more praiseworthy lives.

Of course, flattery is different from praise. Flattery can be insincere and excessive, designed to manipulate or to get something in return. But praise is not manipulative. It is not motivated by the hope that it will be reciprocated.

Praise should be deserved, specific, and sincere. If we look for opportunities to praise, we will find them all around us: in the small, struggling steps of a child, in the improved attitude of a teenager, in the extra effort of a spouse, or in the dedication of a co-worker.

And, in all of us who both give and receive praise, let us not, as the Apostle John has written, love "the praise of men more than the praise of God."[2] Let us strive to glorify and praise God by beginning to praise each other.

....

1. In Elizabeth Longford, *Wellington: The Years of the Sword* (St. Alban's, England: Granada Publishing Ltd., 1976), p. 586.
2. John 12:43.

True Leadership

WHETHER WE REALIZE IT OR NOT, each of us is a leader. At home, at work, in our communities and neighborhoods, we're all involved in the act of leading. We may not hold political office or a formal position of leadership, but we all lead. Every one of us leads our own life, even while we influence those around us.

Leadership is something that can be learned over time, not simply by reading books but also through practice and application. Real leadership comes from a sincere desire to serve, to be true, and to live with integrity. Such strength of character is the trademark of all effective leaders. Consider a great leader who came from inauspicious beginnings. Abraham Lincoln, born in a backwoods cabin, learned from hardship to be strong in the midst of adversity. As a result, he was able to lead and unify a divided nation.

Leadership is more than managing programs and policies; it is first and foremost inspiring people. Businessman Max DePree has written: "In addition to all of the ration and goals and parameters and bottom lines, it is fundamental that leaders endorse a concept of persons. This begins with an understanding of the diversity of people's gifts and talents and skills."[1] Real teamwork is created when leaders value the differences, encourage cooperation and involvement, and recognize that, like them, the people they lead are changing, growing individuals. Whatever our particular role may be—as a leader in a home, organization, or office—the same basic principles apply.

Leadership is an art that requires compassion, empathy, vision, and integrity. True leaders recognize potential and look for greatness. They know themselves and those within their stewardship to be children of God, endowed with infinite power and purpose. They look at their children, spouses, co-workers, constituents, and neighbors not as ordinary people but as members of God's family who all have extraordinary potential. No matter how varied the problems and how diverse the personalities, people—just like you and me—are the real bottom line.

This is the essence of true leadership, and the world cries out for it. We can begin today—right now—to lead with love and believe in others, because we are all leaders.

1. *Leadership Is an Art* (New York: Doubleday, 1989), p. 7.

PART 5

Peace with Self and Others

"To Thine Own Self Be True"

In HANS CHRISTIAN ANDERSEN'S CLASSIC TALE "The Emperor's New Clothes," no one tells the emperor that his new clothes are, in fact, *no* clothes at all. Upon reading the story, we wonder why his courtiers don't tell the truth about his apparel, and we usually conclude that sometimes it is harder to be honest than silent. We close the book with a laugh and a smile and possibly miss another of the story's most telling morals: betraying ourselves is just as wrong as withholding the truth from another person.

The emperor knows all along that his "new robe" is really nonexistent. But because "seeing" the clothing is reputed to be a mark of character, he does not admit—not even to himself—that he actually sees no robe at all. Instead, he questions his own perception and falls prey to the weavers' scandal by pretending to see what he does not. The cycle of lies begins and ends with his failure to be honest with himself.

Self-honesty can sometimes be the most difficult—even painful—truth to tell. We may pride ourselves in being honest with our associates, friends, and family. But are we truly honest with ourselves? Do we sometimes put ourselves up for scrutiny and evaluate who we are and how we are seeing the world? Or are we betrayed by a desire for comfort, not wanting to confront certain character traits, behaviors, attitudes, or issues that are less than pleasant to us? If so, the self-betrayal we cling to may eventually cause more heartache and pain—in ourselves and others—than facing up to flaws and mistakes would.

One noted author and doctor prescribes a balanced diet of self-honesty in order to maintain good mental health. He explains: "We must always hold truth, as best we can determine it, to be more important, more vital to our self-interest, than our comfort."[1] And that means not just being committed to truthful interactions with other people, but first and foremost being honest with ourselves and taking responsibility for our own lives. The emperor had no clothes, not just because his courtiers lied to him, but most important because he was afraid to see himself as he really was.

Self-deception accompanies all other forms of deception. We cannot lie to another person without somehow deceiving ourselves. Shakespeare's wisdom stands the test of time: "This above all: To thine own self be true, / And it must follow, as the night the day, / Thou canst not then be false to any man."[2]

---

1. M. Scott Peck, *The Road Less Traveled* (New York: Simon and Schuster, 1978), p. 51.
2. William Shakespeare, *Hamlet*, act 1, scene 4, lines 77–80.

Strangers to Ourselves

SERVICE IS CENTRAL to Christian living. And yet, incessant demands from friends, family, neighbors, or organizations may fill our lives with more "opportunities" for service than we can really handle. The breathtaking pace required to meet *all* needs may keep us from recognizing our own needs. And, while always looking to others and living for others, we may ignore our own daily requirements for love and service.

Anne Morrow Lindbergh said it this way: "When one is a stranger to oneself then one is estranged from others too. If one is out of touch with oneself, then one cannot touch others."[1]

Whether it be the soothing touch of a parent, the encouraging hug of a friend, or the loving caress of a companion, our ability to reach out to others directly corresponds with our ability to reach into ourselves. For example, airline flight attendants speak of such service every time a plane leaves the ground: "Put your own oxygen mask on first, and then assist children and other passengers" is the standard advice. In the same way, lifeguards keep struggling swimmers afloat because they are themselves good swimmers, equipped with their own life preservers and experienced in their own flotation techniques. Similarly, teachers must fill their own minds with knowledge before they can increase their students' understanding. In other words, we are in a position to help others when we have first helped ourselves.

Only as our own best caretaker can we be the kind of caregiver the Savior describes: "Thou shalt love thy neighbor as thyself."[2] When love of self enhances a love for others, we see what is magical about service. It is a two-way exchange. Parents who build their own emotional muscles have strength to lift a discouraged child. Friends who have goals inspire others to set and achieve goals. Spouses who have forgiven themselves can more readily forgive their companions. An investment in self becomes a deposit for others—with God-given returns.

While service is vitally important to personal development, we can be so busy turning outward that we become afraid or unable to turn inward. And we do ourselves no service. The way to truly turn inward is to get in touch with God. The soul-weary servant will better give love when he or she pauses to feel of the Savior's love. A popular hymn makes this promise poetic: "For I am thy God and will still give thee aid. I'll strengthen thee, help thee, and cause thee to stand . . . upheld by my righteous, omnipotent hand."[3]

Only when we are in a position to be touched by God's all-powerful hand can we really touch others. The circle of our own reach will enlarge when we put ourselves in the hollow of the Lord's hand. But, if we are always looking outward, without looking inward for divine direction and taking time for personal renewal, we may become strangers to ourselves—and to God. Only when we are in touch with God and allow Him to direct our efforts to improve—only when we allow Him to guide our service—can we both feel His love and give it away.

1. *Gift from the Sea* (New York: Random House, 1955), p. 44.

2. Galatians 5:14.

3. "How Firm a Foundation," *Hymns of The Church of Jesus Christ of Latter-day Saints* (Salt Lake City: The Church of Jesus Christ of Latter-day Saints, 1985), no. 85.

Living Outside of Ourselves

ARMAND HAMMER, the well-known industrialist and self-made diplomat, kept a picture of Albert Einstein on the table beside his bed. The first thing he looked at every morning was the inscription below the picture: "A person first starts to live when he can live outside of himself." The genius of this simple wisdom was the guiding force of Mr. Hammer's life—so much so that, when this former chairman of Occidental Petroleum was asked to define the meaning of life, he responded with Einstein's sage counsel: "A person first starts to live when he can live outside of himself." And then he explained in his own words: "I believe we are here to do good . . . , to make the world a better place. . . . Life is a gift, and if we agree to accept it, we must contribute in return. When we fail to contribute, we fail to adequately answer why we are here."[1]

But how can we concern ourselves with others when life—by its nature—may lead us to concentrate only on self? How can we serve our fellow beings when our own happiness—even our survival—seems to demand most of our time and energy? The solution, while ironic, has proven to be true: our own problems, challenges, and responsibilities will somehow seem less weighty as we help to alleviate others' cares. When we begin to live outside of ourselves, we discover how capable of giving we are—and how enjoyable giving is. Health professionals confirm what experience tells us: focusing positively on others will help us feel better about ourselves both mentally and physically. For life truly becomes a gift as we look for opportunities to give of ourselves.

Not long ago, a woman's life took on new meaning when she opened an unexpected note of appreciation. A casual acquaintance had noticed her, felt of her loneliness, and shared of herself. In return, an almost forgotten smile broke through the creases on her face. The woman had been touched by the note in a visible way. And, on that particular day, her newfound smile made its way into someone else's heart. The cycle of caring knows no end as it feeds on sharing and grows on gratitude.

To think that a virtual stranger could make such a difference reminds us of the power we each have to give of ourselves. He who gave us the gift of life knows of such selfless service: "Whosoever shall seek to save his life shall lose it; and whosoever shall lose his life shall preserve it."[2] For no one knows better than the Master Giver that people start to live when they live outside of themselves.

1. David Friend, ed., and the editors of *Life, The Meaning of Life* (Boston: Little, Brown, and Co., 1991), p. 29.
2. Luke 17:33.

The Armor of Light

Each year a miraculous thing happens.

In small, almost imperceptible steps, summer's panorama of vibrant green leaves gives way to a dazzling contrast in the treetops consisting of red, yellow, and orange. Then, almost as if nature is trying to warn the world of the winter ahead, the now brittle and lifeless leaves are soon gone—easily scattered in autumn's cool breezes.

While many suppose this process is due to the cooler temperatures or lack of water, botanists tell us the real culprit is the shortened days, which slowly paralyze the life-giving process of the leaf and its chlorophyll.

The problem, simply put, is the lack of light. Nature, as is often the case, teaches us an invaluable lesson with this annual repainting. It's about light. And, in many ways, it's the same lesson Jesus Christ taught us about light.

But, while nature teaches us using the superior luminescence of the sun as her example, Jesus pointed to a much more common and easily obtainable source of light as being essential for what is almost a kind of photosynthesis in humans.

"Ye are the light of the world," implored the Savior in His Sermon on the Mount. "A city that is set on an hill cannot be hid. Neither do men light a candle and put it under a bushel, but on a candlestick; and it giveth light unto all that are in the house."[1]

Through small and simple acts of service to a family member, a neighbor, the elderly, or even a stranger, mankind is rejuvenated. Humble, flickering, and seemingly insignificant light provides the only bright spot in some people's days. And sometimes this light becomes a lifesaving beacon to those in real darkness.

As Jesus continued, "Let your light so shine before men, that they may see your good works, and glorify your Father which is in heaven."[2]

In today's world, there are as many ways to serve others as there are leaves upon the ground. Sir Francis Child observed, "Every human soul has the germ of some flowers within; and they would open only if they could find some sunshine and free air to expand in. Not having enough sunshine is what ails the world. Make people happy, and there will not be half the quarreling or a tenth part of the wickedness there is."[3]

Through small and simple acts of service, we can indeed diminish much of the darkness in the world—and make the prospects for mankind's future all the brighter.

But the time to do it is now.

As Paul reminded the Romans, "The night is far spent, the day is at hand . . . let us put on the armor of light."[4]

---

1. Matthew 5:14–15.
2. Matthew 5:16.
3. Mark Gilbert, *Wisdom of the Ages* (New York: Garden City Publishing Co., 1936), p. 146.
4. Romans 13:12.

Finding Ourselves in Others

When Jesus instructed His disciples what they should do to demonstrate and develop their love for Him, He said: "Feed my sheep."[1] Again and again, He instructed the apostles that the shortest road to the heart of God leads through the hearts of God's children—our brothers and sisters.

This simple instruction indicates that our salvation is *interdependent* with the lives of those around us. We do not find ourselves only through introspection but through the outward searching of our souls. We discover our own lives and our personalities—indeed, we discover the gift of salvation—through our service and loving and sacrifice for others.

But this simple truth taught by Jesus has been complicated in recent years by the insights of social philosophers. We are told that a common pathology of modern relations is "codependence"—a destructive kind of association that creates a constant, crippling need for other people. Even Christian philosophers have identified this kind of interpersonal needing as an attempt to replace Jesus with other people.

When Jesus directed us to a life of love and service, He did not intend for us to become addicted to the service we perform; He does not want us to define ourselves only by our relationships to other people. Each of us is a child of God. Each of us is a uniquely important creature of His love. Our principal identity springs from that creative fact: He made us; we are His.

But even Jesus longed for the companionship and comfort

and support of friends. And, when He prayed alone in the Garden of Gethsemane, He chastised His disciples for failing to stay awake and support Him with their prayers. As Matthew records, "And he cometh unto the disciples, and findeth them asleep, and saith unto Peter, What, could ye not watch with me one hour?"[2]

With every true principle comes a perversion of the truth, a counterfeit. The truth of human relations is that God desires our interdependence, our participation in one another's lives, our need for love—both the giving and the getting. But the perversion of that truth is a kind of crippling need, a hurtful and destructive appetite incapable of sacrifice or real caring—a kind of selfishness that takes on the name of "love" to justify itself but, in fact, knows only need.

We all have needs. We all need help. But it is not through looking inward to our needs that we find the greatest satisfaction but by looking outward to the lives of others and, through them, to the life-giving love of God.

To believe in the words of Jesus is to know that we cannot find our way home alone. He did not put us here in isolation but as families and communities of caring and interdependent individuals. But, in our loving of one another, we must not lose contact with Him who made and loves us all. If we include God in our relationships, our love of one another will take us home to God.

1. John 21:16.
2. Matthew 26:40.

Age Is Opportunity

SHE IS A WOMAN like many others approaching their seventy-seventh birthday. Arthritis creaks in her joints and tears at her fingers. Operations on her legs and back have left her unable to walk very far. She has lost her husband five years ago; six others of her family have died from cancer. In short, like many others, she has experienced tragedy enough to give up on life and end up bitter or despondent.

But the remarkable thing about her is what she does in spite of her years, in spite of the pain, in spite of the dozens of reasons she could simply surrender.

In the past decade, she has made hundreds of quilts—first for her children (grand and great) and next for every newborn in the neighborhood. Last year, she helped make one hundred quilts, which were sent to a hospital in Nicaragua.

She donates time at a sheltered workshop for the handicapped. She is compiling a book documenting the lives of her ancestors. She brings meals to her invalid friends and drives them to their doctors' offices.

"I see people," she says, "who have just given up. Maybe they have reasons—heaven knows there are enough of them—but they've stopped even wanting to live.

"There is always beauty in the world if you want to look for it," she'll tell you with a smile, "and, besides, I'm not giving up as long as I see somebody else going."

The French philosopher Montaigne wrote that the value of

life lies not in the length of days but in the use we make of them; a person may live long yet live very little.

Longfellow put it this way:

> The night hath not yet come; we are not quite
> Cut off from labor by the failing light;
> Something remains for us to do or dare;
> Even the oldest tree some fruit may bear
>
> . . . .
>
> For age is opportunity no less
> Than youth itself, though in another dress.
> And as the evening twilight fades away
> The sky is filled with stars, invisible by day.[1]

It's inevitable that life will test us with our own heartaches and burdens. But, when we arrive at the point where surrender seems more desirable than fighting against depression and pain, remember a seventy-six-year-old woman who, through acts of simple kindness, has discovered the secret to a life of purpose and contribution.

She and many like her teach through example what instinctively we all know to be true: no matter how old we are, age is opportunity.

1. "Morituri Salutamus," *The Complete Poetical Works of Longfellow* (Boston: Houghton Mifflin Company, 1922), p. 314.

Bearing Our Burdens;
Cheering Our Hearts

WHEN THE POET WROTE: "Father, cheer our souls tonight; lift our burdens, make them light,"[1] both hope and supplication were expressed. But, for us to appreciate the sincerity of that hope and the necessity of the request, we must first recognize the reality of the need. There are nights in which our souls are cheerless, our burdens heavier than we know how to bear.

On such occasions, the companionship of Jesus may seem very far away. We may even be tempted to wonder what good is the scope and sweep of salvation, when what we really need is someone to hold our hand—someone to offer solutions to our immediate problems.

Perhaps our children are not behaving as they should. Our job may not be going right. We may have bills to pay and people disappointed in our performance. The car may be broken down, the plumbing backed up, and the garden infested with snails. On such occasions, of what use is Jesus?

Well, heavenly resources may not provide immediate solutions for day-to-day troubles. We may have to suffer snails in our gardens from time to time. But the influence of Jesus Christ, both directly and indirectly, touches everything we do. The direct influence of His love and help and hope may come in the comfort we receive from prayer and the direction that comes through inspiration. And the indirect influence of Jesus may be experienced through the help we receive from friends and loved ones.

One of the reasons we were not put on earth one at a time is so that we may provide resources for one another. Sometimes that means someone will come to help us clear a clogged drain, and sometimes it means someone will just sit with us and fret and worry about the things we cannot help. Our burdens need not always be lifted to be made lighter by the love we feel from family and friends.

Does this association and reliance mean we are not independent? No; it only means *we are not alone.* We still must seek Jesus and find Him for ourselves. We still must take responsibility for our action and inaction. We still must exercise faith and find answers to our prayers within those associations blessed by God.

Where is Jesus when we need Him? He is *where* we need him, always. And the manifestations of His love and hope and help are everywhere in our lives. Even when our problems are problems still, even when the solution to our trouble is not so speedy nor certain as we had asked, even when the cheerless nights continue dark—Jesus is our Savior, still.

....

1. Ellis Reynolds Shipp, "Father, Cheer Our Souls Tonight," *Hymnal Plus,* Book 5 (Orem, Utah: Sonos, 1986), p. 38.

Finding Yourself

WE ALL HAVE THE FEAR of losing something, and often our fears are realized. We lose money on the stock market; we lose our wallet at the ball game; we misplace our car keys, mislay important papers. Losing things just seems to be a daily activity for most of us.

While losing things can be inconvenient, frustrating, or even discouraging, there is one loss that is tragic—the loss of ourselves.

Ironically, this greatest of all losses is many times the easiest to accomplish. The fact is, in this computerized, hectic, mechanized world we have made, it is quite easy to misplace ourselves.

To lose one's self is to lose touch with our feelings, to wander away from our own personality; it is to become a stranger to what is essentially us—our inner spirit, our thoughts, our emotions, the sensation of self.

The person who has lost himself lives solely for things, or for others, reacting only to outside demands and pressures. Of course, service to others is commendable; but servitude is not service.

The businessman, for example, who spends all of his waking hours with his career—with flow charts, marketing surveys, contracts—responding hour by hour, day by day to the continuous demands of work, has lost himself. Similarly, parents who devote all of their waking hours to children with never a thought for themselves—their development, their happiness, their needs— have lost themselves. The better we take care of ourselves, the better we are able to care for others. Happiness, self-fulfillment, emotional health are dependent upon staying in touch with ourselves.

Losing one's self is not only self-destructive, but it can also be harmful to others around us. But, for those of us who have lost a portion of ourselves, the following advice may be helpful.

Spend some time alone each day. It may not be fashionable, but it is therapeutic. Let your mind think what it wants to; do a little daydreaming. Walt Disney called it "imagineering"—vividly imagining and visually engineering the creation and realization of your dreams.

Pamper yourself. Take a day off when you feel yourself going under. Step out of the rat race when you need to.

Follow at least one dream. Take up the violin; become an amateur astronomer; search for fossils in the desert; refinish antique rocking chairs; enroll in an art class.

Value yourself. Feel blessed in your gifts and accomplishments. Don't be afraid to respectfully express your opinion and say no to unrealistic demands placed on you by others.

You are your most valuable possession. Take time to find yourself.

Removing Rocks

....

Year after year, an old farmer planted and plowed around a large rock in his field. Even after breaking several plowshares and a cultivator against the stone, he continued to work around it. He grew rather accustomed to this enemy in the field. And then one day he lost another plowshare to the rock. Remembering all the problems it had caused him through the years, he finally decided to take action. Putting a crowbar under the stone, he discovered that the "foreboding rock" was only a few inches thick and could easily be broken with a sledgehammer. Hauling the crushed pieces away, he smiled sadly as he reflected on all the trouble the rock had given him and how he could have gotten rid of it years ago.

His life's labor was much easier now that the rock had been removed. And life for each of us can be much easier when we remove rocks of pride, stones of resentment, and boulders of bitterness. If we refuse to face such rocks, they may actually get bigger over time. The more our habits entrench them, the more difficult they are to remove. When we arrogantly shun forgiveness or spitefully hold on to slights, these pebbles of pride will slowly evolve into self-destructing stones of anger, even monuments to our malice.

Only after we apply the hammer of humility can we feel the force of forgiveness and experience the freedom of letting go. We need the crowbar to wedge beneath weaknesses, face faults, and get past grudges. Some rocks may be difficult, if not impossible, to remove—at least on our own. They can be more than one life wide, spanning several generations.

The challenge is to sincerely face the boulders in our lives and responsibly—even prayerfully—do what we can do to remove them. God knows the deepest parts of our hearts, and He can help us keep them sensitive and open even while the stones of silence, the rocks of misery, the pebbles of pain would close them.

Solutions may not always be easy. It's difficult to remove hardened rocks. But it's just as troublesome to work around them. Life is so much easier, so much more enjoyable, when our soul is emptied of destructive stones.

"The Great Sin"

THERE IS ONE VICE of which no [person] in the world is free," wrote C. S. Lewis, "which everyone in the world loathes when he [or she] sees it in someone else; and of which hardly any people . . . ever imagine that they are guilty themselves. . . . There is no fault which makes a [person] more unpopular, and no fault which we are more unconscious of in ourselves. And the more we have it ourselves, the more we dislike it in others."[1] Lewis was referring to pride, or self-conceit, and he called it "The Great Sin."

Indeed, pride has been the chief cause of misery since the world began: causing families to disintegrate, marriages to break up, and neighborhoods and nations to fight. Pride is characterized by consuming self-interest, compulsive competitiveness, and encompassing envy. And it can be so deceptive. While our intentions may seem sincere and our cause may be worthy, our attitude may be arrogant and our motives self-serving. Do we perform well at work, contribute in our community, and serve our family because we want to look good and be popular? Or are we putting forth extra efforts, volunteering our talents, and spending time with our family because we really care?

Pride would have us adopt a "me-first" mentality, closing our eyes to everything but a shallow reflection in a one-way mirror. Pride confuses conceit for self-esteem and considers humility and meekness to be weak. Such is the falsity of arrogance.

But true self-esteem is manifestly forgiving, nonjudgmental, and gracious. With real confidence, we shun self-conceit and look to God with humble gratitude. C. S. Lewis concludes: "As long as you are proud you cannot know God. A proud man is always looking down on things and people: and, of course, as long as you are looking down, you cannot see something that is above you."[2]

In our day and age, no message is more important. We must replace pride with humility and self-conceit with Godly dependence, for pride will only deaden our compassion, destroy our sensitivity, and deceive us with vanity.

As was said long ago, "God resisteth the proud, but giveth grace unto the humble."[3]

1. *Mere Christianity* (New York: Macmillan, 1952), p. 108–9.
2. Ibid., p. 104.
3. James 4:6.

The Peace of Forgiveness

A PERSON'S ABILITY TO FORGIVE is in proportion to the greatness of his soul. Little men [and women] cannot forgive," said a wise observer. Proud and petty people cannot forgive; neither can the stubborn and selfish. Only the humble, meek, and penitent are able to let go of offenses and grant sincere pardons. Truly, how we respond to wrongs—real or imagined—reveals our character.

Few things can be as difficult as forgiving someone who has offended, betrayed, or let us down. We all have reasons to take offense; but are we "offender[s] for a word," upset by small slights, attuned to unfairness, offended even when no offense was intended?[1] Perhaps we say that someone else is at fault—and that may be true—but do we maintain our own climate of injustice? Do we spend a day, a year, a lifetime being so "right" that, eventually, we become wrong?

While we justify an unforgiving attitude and wallow in pride, grudges grow, feelings of resentment fester, and relationships may be destroyed.

"How difficult it is for any of us to forgive those who have injured us," wrote Gordon B. Hinckley. "We are all prone to brood on the evil done us. That brooding becomes as a gnawing and destructive canker. Is there a virtue more in need of application in our time than the virtue of forgiving and forgetting? There are those who would look upon this as a sign of weakness. . . . [But] it takes neither strength nor intelligence to brood in anger over wrongs suffered, to go through life with a spirit of vindictiveness, to dissipate one's abilities in planning retribution. There is no peace in the nursing of a grudge. There is no happiness in living for the day when you can 'get even.'"[2]

"The peace of God, which passeth all understanding,"[3] is promised to those who truly forgive. In our quest for peace, we may not always be able to make good with the offender, for we cannot force forgiveness or demand repentance. But we can make right with ourselves when we let go of wrongs and look to God for comfort. As we do so, our relationships will improve, our joy in life will expand, and we will have peace of mind.

Right now, we can resolve to forgive, determine to forget, decide to move forward.

1. Isaiah 29:21.
2. "Of You It Is Required to Forgive," *Ensign*, June 1991, p. 4.
3. Philippians 4:7.

Forgiving Yourself

In a candid moment born of fatigue, a loving, conscientious mother of five lively children confessed to her teenage son that she had always found it very difficult to admit her mistakes. She knew she was slow to acknowledge when she was at fault—slow to offer apology to the family and friends she adored.

The wisdom of the boy's response surprised her: "Maybe you have a hard time forgiving yourself," he said.

This young man correctly perceived that the pain of making mistakes may cause us to avoid confronting our errors. It is as though we feel we cannot possibly be worthwhile if we are less than perfect. And yet, as the Greek dramatist Euripides noted, "Men are men, they needs must err."[1] To be human, almost by definition, means that we will sometimes stumble.

How wonderful is the practice of self-forgiveness then! Self-forgiveness is the assurance that we are still valuable in spite of our errors. Self-forgiveness is permission to get up, dust ourselves off, and try it again. Self-forgiveness is the psychological equivalent of a second chance.

The benefits of forgiving ourselves are many. When we forgive ourselves for our own shortcomings, we actually take an important step toward overcoming them. We can acknowledge our faults and move to correct them instead of becoming paralyzed by a sense of our inadequacy.

When we forgive ourselves for our own weaknesses, we greet the people in our lives with tolerant hearts. Responding to our

171

friends and family members with an attitude of acceptance, rather than accusations, creates a climate of trust and warmth in which relationships can flourish.

And finally, when we freely forgive ourselves and others, we invite a spirit of peace to reside with us—the kind of divine peace celebrated in song: "There'll be love and forgiveness, there'll be peace and contentment, there'll be joy, joy, joy."[2]

1. In Robert I. Fitzhenry, ed., *The Harper Book of Quotations*, 3rd ed. (New York: HarperCollins, 1993), p. 301.
2. Natalie Sleeth, "Joy in the Morning," published by Hope Publishing Co.

Personal Responsibility

BLAMING OTHERS for everything that has happened in the past, everything that troubles us now, and everything that will upset us in the future has become a popular pastime. All too often, we see ourselves as victims, merely surviving in the midst of circumstances over which we think we have no control. We may create scapegoats of all sorts to swallow personal responsibility. And we may find ourselves thinking, "If only I had different parents," "If only I'd been born in another city or gone to another school," "If only I looked different," "If only I had more money," and so on. The "if onlys" of life temporarily relieve us of responsibility and allow us to think that we do not make choices for ourselves.

While we may explain away those parts of our life with which we are not satisfied, we can never really change our circumstances unless we change our focus. As long as we search "out there" for all of the solutions to our problems, we may neglect the great power within each of us to take action and be responsible. Brian Tracy explains: "All negative emotions tend to be associated with blame. Fully 99 percent of all our problems exist only because we're able to blame someone or something for them. The instant we stop blaming, our negative emotions begin disappearing."[1]

That does not mean that past hurts and disadvantages are not real; nor does it mean that life is easy and everything will go our way. Our backgrounds and circumstances may be less than ideal—our struggles serious. But we need not be victims of conditions or conditioning. We can determine our destiny, decide our direction, chart our course, and choose a path for ourselves, for the Lord has said that every person is accountable, as a steward, over "earthly blessings" and—we might add—over earthly trials and troubles as well.[2]

The real challenge of life is to take what we have been born with—both the good and the bad—to stop blaming and making excuses and to create a pocket of excellence where we are. We can all change, grow, and start anew throughout our lives. As we take personal responsibility and look to God for guidance and comfort, we will find inside ourselves great strength—even God-given power—to make good choices, to forgive others, and to move forward.

1. Brian Tracy, *Insight*, no. 112, p. 16.
2. Doctrines and Covenants, 104:13.

A Lasting Mark

THE ITALIAN VIOLIN MAKER Antonio Stradivari died in the year 1737 at ninety-three years of age. The average life expectancy at that time was not much over thirty years. Stradivari's passion produced over a thousand instruments during his lifetime, and his workmanship brought the violin to perfection. He was self-taught and usually worked alone until, late in life, his sons joined him in the craft.

Although Stradivari's tools were primitive, his artistry was exquisite. When he finished with an instrument and was satisfied with its quality, he would sign his name on the violin. Today, more than 250 years later, a Stradivarius violin is still known through the world as the epitome of craftsmanship. Stradivari's commitment to excellence and quality is legendary.[1]

While few of us may be in the business of making musical instruments, we are all involved in the act of creating. Are we willing to proudly put our name on our work in hopes that it, too, will stand the test of time?

Without even knowing it, we leave our signature on people, projects, and places throughout our life. An ancient Chinese proverb tells us: "A child's life is like a piece of paper on which every passerby leaves a mark." It's no different with adults. Like Stradivari, devoted parents leave their mark; they're creators, providing guidance and love. Dedicated teachers are builders, encouraging dreams and aspirations. And true friends are motivators,

175

extending support and comfort. All these live on for countless generations in the hearts and minds of their recipients.

When we strive for quality in our interpersonal relationships and excellence in our personal life, we leave a lasting mark. Our name will be held in honorable remembrance from generation to generation. The Proverbs quite simply teach us that "a good name is rather to be chosen than great riches, and loving favour rather than silver and gold."[2] This is the kind of lasting influence that matters—the kind that stands the test of time.

1. Denis Waitley, *The Double Win* (New York: Berkeley, 1986), p. 93.
2. Proverbs 22:1.

Aspirations and Ambitions

Henry Ward Beecher once described ambition as a vulgar form of aspiration.[1] The definitions may be debatable, but the difference he points out is profound. There is within each of us a divinely placed desire to raise ourselves above our present levels. The desire is universal, but the way we fulfill that desire can take us to a path of self-improvement and fulfillment, or down to depths of frustration, jealousy, and bitterness.

When we aspire properly we try to improve our performance—not for the applause and glory it may bring us, but because it will make us more effective in the service of others. In our work we are more concerned about how well we serve than how well we are paid. In our volunteer service we are more focused on what is accomplished than on who gets the credit.

To aspire in the best sense means lifting the lives of those about us. It means cheering more for the successes of others than for our own accomplishments.

The finest example of noble aspirations was Jesus Christ. He acknowledged His high calling and fulfilled it to the fullest. Yet, He was always the humble servant: willing to share His bread with the beggar and wash the feet of His disciples. He gave us the formula for the highest form of aspiring when He said, "But he that is greatest among you shall be your servant. And whosoever shall exalt himself shall be abased; and he that shall humble himself shall be exalted."[2]

Humbly aspiring to do our best brings us the joy of knowing we have left others better for having known us.

Vulgar ambition, on the other hand, leads down a road of self-glorification. Selfishly ambitious people are always looking out for number one. They are always concerned and conscious about whether they are receiving the money, acclaim, and fame they think they deserve. And, always they hunger for more, for the appetite of ambition is bottomless. It grows on what it consumes. It turns people into insatiable consumers of the world's goods and glory, and there is never enough.

Our attitude in ambition and aspiration determines whether we go hungrily or happily through life. The whole world has not sufficient to feed the hungry ambitions of the vainglorious person.

On the other hand, when we aspire to be better so we can serve better, we find abundance all around us. There is satisfying work to be done. There are grateful recipients of our gifts, and faithful friends from our labors. Our lives are rich and full.

Let us overcome vulgar ambition with lofty aspirations. Let us overcome our best selves and use our abilities to bless the lives of others. That is a mountain worth climbing—a dream worth achieving.

....

1. In *Instant Quotation Dictionary* (Little Falls, New Jersey: Donald O. Bolander Co. Career Institute, 1972), p. 16.
2. Matthew 23:11–12.

Something to Share

It is still a marvel that a collection of men and women from diverse cultures and homes could come together, share a vision, and give birth to a new nation such as the United States of America. Often, when we celebrate this country, we speak of the stubborn independence of our forefathers that made it all possible. Yet, just as remarkable is the profound cooperation at the heart of it all.

There, in Independence Hall—with the heat and flies of summer, the doors locked, and the windows bolted—sat a group of men who decided together to commit treason against their motherland and sign the Declaration of Independence. It was not just faith in their ideals they were asserting but faith in each other—faith that in the long struggle ahead they could count on each other, look to each other, bear one another's burdens.

Without that spirit of cooperation among people, nothing really great ever happens. Even when an idea begins with one person, it is in their connectedness that people start movements, change the course of history, and bless each other.

George Washington didn't win the Revolutionary War alone. He did it with the cooperation of thousands of ordinary people willing to go sometimes without food. And these soldiers didn't fight only for themselves. They fought for families in cabins in New England or on farms in Virginia. They fought for generations yet unborn whom they would never see.

Even when settlers moved west, they came in wagon trains

to strengthen each other, feeding each other when provisions were low, nursing each other through sickness. No wilderness could have been tamed by a single person.

Yet, it is the great tendency of our time to lose sight of our connectedness with each other. The Lord has said that the crowning attribute of His people is that they are "of one heart,"[1] but too often we see each other as competitors for a limited prize. We come to believe in survival of the fittest, where every man prospers according to his genius, and every man conquers according to his strength.

With such a belief, we learn to see each other with hostility instead of connection. We pit our intellects, opinions, works, wealth, and talent against each other, seeing the other person as someone to best. As C. S. Lewis said, "Pride gets no pleasure out of having something, only out of having more of it than the next man. . . . It is the comparison that makes you proud: the pleasure of being above the rest."[2]

This self-serving view that divides us from others did not give birth to this nation. It was connectedness, not competition, that brought us together. It was a people seeing what they shared, willing to sacrifice for their dream and for each other. It is only this same spirit that can move us forward again. Today, we know what our problems are, but we must also see clearly what our legacy is. In America, we have something we share that is worth holding onto; and, when we hold onto each other, we can succeed.

1. Moses 7:18.
2. *Mere Christianity* (New York: Macmillan, 1952), pp. 109–10.

A Perspective on Patriotism

WHETHER STIRRED by a ringing anthem or a silent reflection, most of us, no doubt, have thanked God for the blessings of a free land—for our freedom of thought and deed.

We take understandable pride in our ability to shape our own lives, to chart an individual course. Indeed, our freedom to choose is viewed by many not only as an inalienable right but as the greatest of all God's gifts.

Yet freedom, said Peter Marshall, "is not the right to do as one pleases but the opportunity to please do what is right."[1] Therein lies the paradox of our agency: To be truly free, we must transcend our own self-interests and consider the effect of our actions on family, friends, and the multitudes we may never meet. Community, then, is born of an interest in the common good, in the exercise of our freedom for the benefit of something larger than our little corner of the world.

"Our best use of freedom," wrote Dr. O. C. Tanner, "is to [be] . . . free *for* and not *from* something. To be sure, we want to be free from the will and enslavement of others," he continued. "But that is only half of the matter; we then must find some loyalty that makes us truly free—the cause of truth, the enlargement of mental horizons, the creation of beauty, and a community made better for all because we are living there."[2]

Each is free to choose the contributions he or she will make—and, sadly, some choose to make none—but no country, no matter how large or wealthy or influential, will ever be greater than the collective goodness of its individual citizens.

Therein lies the true measure of commitment to country— the all too often unheralded devotion to interests larger than our own. God has, indeed, given us the blessing of freedom—and a country committed to its preservation. What we now do with that freedom—how we use the gift we have been given—becomes the real measure of our patriotism.

And, given our debt to God, we would be wise to seek His help and guidance as we work to make our difference in the world. In the words of the hymn,

> The Lord be with us as we walk
> Along our homeward road.
> In silent thought or friendly talk,
> Our hearts be near to God.[3]

---

1. In Emerson R. West, comp., *Vital Quotations* (Salt Lake City: Bookcraft, 1968), p. 123.
2. Obert C. Tanner, *Christ's Ideals for Living* (Salt Lake City: Deseret Sunday School Union Board, 1955), p. 344.
3. "The Lord Be with Us," *Hymns of The Church of Jesus Christ of Latter-day Saints* (Salt Lake City: The Church of Jesus Christ of Latter-day Saints, 1985), no. 161.

The Ensign of the Nation

KEEP YOUR EYE on the grand old flag . . . , the emblem of the land I love, the home of the free and the brave."[1] We honor our flag with songs, salutes, and celebrations. But the real meaning of the nation's ensign is written on the hearts and minds of its citizens. Held high by more than a steel pole, the flag flies so long as we uphold all for which it stands.

As one editorial reads, "[The flag has] inspired countless soldiers to defend freedom in various places worldwide. It was planted in the fine dust of the moon as a symbol of dreams that can become reality. . . . And . . . [it has flown] over thousands of graves . . . as a reminder of the sacrifices that freedom often requires of its benefactors."[2]

A flag is such a powerful symbol, so much more than just a piece of cloth. For as long as battles have been fought, flags have been raised to represent ideals. They inspire devotion and dreams, they represent loyalties and sacrifice, and they may symbolize freedom and opportunity for people worldwide. Perhaps their threads are laced with pain for some, but of those very strands, pride and betterment are usually born. School children, athletes, soldiers, and silent patriots across the land pledge allegiance to flags.

But what does this age-old symbol mean to you personally? Does it prompt thoughts of what's right with your land and life? Does it inspire a lifestyle that reflects its ideals? Does it motivate you to prosper the land you love? Do you display it proudly and often, understanding that living beneath its shadow can be a blessing beyond measure?

In days of peace our duty is just as important as in more tumultuous times. The threats may be more subtle, but they are still being waged. The challenges may be different, but they are there to be faced. And all the while, the flag flies, inspiring us to do our part, reminding us that its power, its life-preserving purpose, even its God-given opportunities must be cherished in the hearts and minds of the people.

1. George M. Cohen, "You're a Grand Old Flag."
2. *Deseret News,* June 13, 1994, p. A8.

The Fight for Freedom

THE LAST MONTH OF 1776 was especially difficult for the American troops fighting for independence. The nights were colder, the sick lists longer, and the army near disintegration. With the onset of winter, General Washington could count only about six thousand troops ready—yet scarcely fit—for duty. In contrast to the bold and proud spirit of the preceding summer, few glimmers of hope now transcended the barriers of war and winter.[1]

It was during this bleak period, just months after the Declaration of Independence had been signed, that Thomas Paine began publishing a series of pamphlets appropriately called *The Crisis*. The pamphlets were read to Washington's troops and did much to boost the morale of soldiers and citizens alike. "These are the times that try men's souls," Paine so timelessly wrote. "The summer soldier and the sunshine patriot will, in this crisis, shrink from the service of their country; but he that stands it now, deserves the love and thanks of man and woman. . . . The harder the conflict, the more glorious the triumph. What we obtain too cheap, we esteem too lightly; it is dearness only that gives everything its value. Heaven knows how to put a proper price upon its goods; and it would be strange indeed if so celestial an article as freedom should not be highly rated."[2]

Paine may well have described our time as one that tries men's and women's souls. While the challenges are different, the rewards of justice and liberty are still hard-won. And yet, how apathetic many of us have become toward the cause of freedom.

Perhaps it is even easier to be a "summer soldier and a sunshine patriot" in this age, when freedoms have been showered upon us. Let us remember that—though battles were won—the war for liberty continues.

Do we uphold our freedom by complying with laws? Do we advance the cause of justice by being honest and fair in our dealings? Do we value the wars our forefathers fought by appreciating "life, liberty, and the pursuit of happiness"? These are lofty questions, to be sure. But the answers are acted out in our day-to-day lives: in the way we observe laws, interact with our fellow citizens, and involve ourselves in the democratic process.

As Hugh B. Brown observed, "If you claim the rights of freedom, you must undertake to assume its duties and responsibilities. Freedom is a test of will, a trial of moral strength.[3]

We value our liberties by remembering the battles of yesterday and by being responsible citizens today; for those freedoms we have obtained so dearly, we must not esteem too lightly.

....

1.James L. Stokebury, *A Short History of the American Revolution* (New York: William Morrow and Company, 1991), pp. 114–15.
2. "The Crisis, No. 1," *The Norton Anthology of American Literature*, 2nd ed. (New York: W. W. Norton & Company, 1986), p. 221.
3. Hugh B. Brown, *Eternal Quest*, edited by Charles Manley Brown (Salt Lake City: Bookcraft, 1956), p. 339.

PART 6

The Peace of Family and Friends

The Braided Cord of Humanity

Reflect for a moment upon those who have gone before you. Pause to remember—or at least to imagine—the lives, struggles, sacrifices, and glories of your ancestors. Find out about your parents, grandparents, and great-grandparents, too. For, as Russell Baker has written, "We all come from the past, and children ought to know what it was that went into their making, to know that life is a braided cord of humanity stretching up from time long gone, and that it cannot be defined by the span of a single journey."[1]

As we become familiar with our individual origins, we realize that none of us is on a "single journey." The anecdotes we recall and the histories we uncover may seem strangely familiar, even while they are each unique. We may encounter friends within the parched pages of journals and weathered photographs of family histories. Or, on the other hand, we may seem to find little in common with the men and women who make up our past. No matter how similar or different they are from us, the vital threads that bind our lives together—the cords that link our present to their past—come together to form a rich tapestry that is none other than God's handiwork.

We can be assured that those people who have gone before us are somehow part of us today. We may not understand just now why God gave us our unique sets of ancestors—or maybe even why we were born to our particular parents. But we do know that they are part of us and that, as we learn more about them, we'll better appreciate why we are connected to them. Such weaving of family threads or, as Malachi phrased it, turning of "the heart[s] of the fathers to the children, and the heart[s] of the children to their fathers," not only links us with our kindred dead but also leads us to our Heavenly Father.[2] For He is the Master Weaver and, with His help, we can gather the loose ends and strengthen the eternal ties that hold families together.

When we think about this "braided cord of humanity" that ties one generation to another, we realize that, no matter how imperfect and flawed that cord may be, it *is* divinely inspired. We are connected to our parents, grandparents, and kindred dead for reasons that may be greater than our ability to understand. We are families because God made us so.

....

1. *Growing Up* (New York: Congdon and Weed, 1982), p. 8.
2. Malachi 4:6.

The Little Moments

MANY OF US hold dear the memories of our childhood: school days with friends, our first bicycle, the tree house we helped to build.

But we also may remember those moments that at the time didn't seem particularly significant, such as having a pizza and picnics with Mom or summer hikes with Dad. We may remember those little moments for one reason—they were times spent with our parents.

As we struggle through life, do we purposely take the time to give our children memories they will cherish—not the grand, expensive items and events they seem to want, but the simple, small moments of our time, our friendship?

One mother of six children learned that it was the one-on-one time spent with each child that meant the most and had the greatest influence on her children when they were grown. It was the little moments of reading a favorite book with each child, walking around the block, or taking one child at a time to the grocery store that seemed to matter most.

We, too, can spend one-on-one moments with our children. For that moment, while your child is the only one with you, he or she doesn't have to share you with the world. For that moment, there is no competition for your affection. For that moment, your son or daughter feels as though he or she is the most important person in the world to you.

Remembering the many times his father took him to work, a

young man, now a father himself, took his son to work with him on occasion. One morning, on the way to work, this tender, impressionable son looked at his father and said, "Dad, you've got to be the best dad in the world!" Nothing meant more to that father than this reassuring declaration by his son. In the son's eyes, time spent with his father was truly grand. Surely, the boy will remember the one-on-one times with his father well into adulthood and will perhaps one day do the same with his own children. As we remember those little moments shared with our parents, we, too, can strive to make time to give our children memories they will always cherish.

Family Relationships

WE OFTEN ASSUME that family relationships are the responsibility of parents, but harmony in the home is a two-way street, and children have to do their part as well.

Some children may regard themselves only as biological offspring, without any responsibility to parents. They feel parents have an obligation to respond to their every whim and wish and demand that all must be equal among siblings. Favoritism has no place in the family circle, but, surely, circumstances can bring different parental responses.

Behavior occurs in patterns, and it is not uncommon for families to experience cycles of conflicts, mood changes, or failed communication. When there are problems, we are all at fault because our individual behaviors fit together and feed on each other. But on an individual level, each family member is responsible for his or her choices. This characteristic of interconnectedness makes the family a unique system, but it also means that change in one or more parts of the family is usually accompanied by change in other parts.

It's also possible for a family to have too much closeness. Members can have a powerful sense of belonging and feel great to be together, but they shouldn't give up their individual autonomy.

All family members need to be well acquainted with the law of consequences—of cause and effect. We have to obey financial truths if we want to prosper. We have to obey laws of the land or society will crumble. The law of consequences is one of the most basic principles of heaven and earth, and it can be applied to virtually every aspect of our lives.

All family members share the responsibility of family relationships. And as children grow up and leave home, they must do their part to nurture parental relationships: visits, phone calls, remembering special occasions, keeping in touch.

Today when family life is being challenged, we need to emphasize more than ever the absolutely essential nature of the family as an institution of civilization—as the foundation of nations.

When a family functions well, it can be a never-ending source of love, strength, and growth for its members. Strong family relationships provide a long and rich harvest. And what greater fruit than strong family bonds as we grow older together. Good family life is the ultimate joy of our existence, for where our treasures are, there will our hearts be also.

Successful Marriage

PERHAPS THE GREATEST SOCIAL CHANGE from our parents' generation until today has been the dramatic rise in the divorce rate. A recent study showed that more than half of all first marriages now end in divorce.[1] Certainly our world is different from the world our parents grew up in. High stress, demanding professions, and conflicting schedules all work together to create conflict in our lives.

But, while lifestyles may change, the blueprint for successful and lasting marriages remains the same.

David O. McKay listed three ideals that contribute to the success of a marriage. He first listed loyalty—to put each other first and foremost in all aspects of a marriage. Second, to have self-control. When harsh words or critical remarks come to mind, show restraint. The result is greater love and peace in the home. And third, courtesy—to treat each other every day as though you were still dating.[2]

Richard L. Evans wrote: "Marriage requires the giving and keeping of confidences, the sharing of thoughts and feelings, unfailing respect and understanding, and a frank and gentle communication."[3]

These ideals sound so simple and easy to put into practice, but each day marriages fail because the simple and seemingly insignificant things are overlooked.

There is no such thing as a marriage that can't be strengthened, and the best time to start is today. Take a moment to say, "I love you." Fix a favorite dinner. Send flowers for no reason. Write a love note. Read a poem together or watch your favorite movie. Tell each other you'd do it all over again.

Yes, it is possible to have a marriage that lasts in today's world. And a successful marriage isn't always strengthened by the big things. More often, it's strengthened by the little things.

1. "The American Family, 1992," *Fortune,* August 10, 1992, p. 43.
2. In Hugh B. Brown, *You and Your Marriage* (Salt Lake City: Bookcraft, 1960), pp. 96–97.
3. "Message of Inspiration," *Church News,* August 15, 1992, p. 2.

Gratitude for Parents

SHAKESPEARE DESCRIBED the biting pain of ingratitude to parents with these words: "How sharper than a serpent's tooth it is to have a thankless child!"[1] And he was right. Of all the injuries suffered by parents, ingratitude hurts the most.

The truth is that most parents can weather many child-rearing difficulties: sickness, failures at school, trauma over boyfriends and girlfriends, financial problems, possible divorce, and subsequent challenges with grandchildren—all of the demands of modern-day parenthood—as long as children are grateful.

As all of us are children, all of us should be grateful. There are very few of us who do not owe some debt of gratitude to our parents. And, in most cases, the debt is great. Think back to childhood—to the bedtime stories, to the bandages on scraped knees, to a mother's kiss of assurance as nighttime shadows closed in, to a father's quiet nod of assurance from the bleachers at the little league park.

Virtually every child has been the joy of his mother, the pride of his father. And, for most parents, that joy and pride has required sacrifice and duty.

All too often, we as children withhold our gratitude, our thanks, even our affection from parents. Our rationale varies: sometimes we blame our own weaknesses or failures on our parents; some of us feel that parental duty is a social responsibility that requires no gratitude; and others of us are simply selfish and ungrateful by nature.

But, whatever cause we harbor for failure to express appreciation to our parents, ingratitude is never justified.

Gratitude is the only pay parents receive for their years of service—service that continues in most cases until life itself ceases.

Perhaps the greatest ingratitude of all is post-mortem appreciation—that given at the graveside. The eulogies, the wreaths, the epitaphs do little to bless our parents' lives. Now is the time to thank our parents for their unconditional gift of life and love—now, while their ears can hear; now, while their hearts can thrill and be made happier with the sweet words of gratitude.

Let our eulogies to parents be written upon the fleshy chambers of living hearts. Let our wreaths be gentle words and caresses placed about the necks of those who can still appreciate their fragrance.

Let us be swift to appreciate parents—while there is time.

1. In Burton Stevenson, comp., *The Home Book of Quotations* (New York: Dodd, Mead, & Co., 1934), p. 984.

Blessed Mothers

In THIS COUNTRY, and in many others, a special day is set aside—a kind of assurance that the mothers of the world won't be forgotten. Mother's Day is the second Sunday in May, and it is now as much a part of the American heritage as Thanksgiving or the Fourth of July.

Motherhood is far more than procreation. It is a holy calling—a sacred dedication and devotion to the rearing, fostering, and nurturing of body, mind, and spirit. It demands all the high virtues, all the strong traits of character required to mold human life into a Christlike pattern.

In Proverbs we find, "Train up a child in the way he should go; and when he is old, he will not depart from it."[1] Those are the words of a very wise and inspired man. Could there be a more sacred responsibility than to be a trustee for honorable, well-born, well-developed children?

Motherhood is not easy. Mothers have their trials—days when the glorious mantle of motherhood feels far away. The responsibility is challenging, especially in today's complex world. There are economic pressures, social pressures, and the constant worry that harmful habits may infect our children.

But time doesn't change basic principles. A child's first relationship is with his or her mother, and it is within this relationship that attitudes are formed. A good relationship will enable a child to accept setbacks without feeling personally attacked. Mothers help teach tolerance and goodwill and respect for the rights of others. And, in many cases, the standards of ethics learned gradually from a mother will determine a child's morality and his or her stature as a human being. Mothers are the master teachers, because they are the first and most vital influence in a child's life.

Mothers are blessed as they struggle with the challenges of rearing children—praying always, believing in the potential of each child, never giving up, and doing all they do with love unfeigned. The product of all their effort is good children. There is no experience more fulfilling or rewarding.

Mothers usually ask for nothing, but they deserve much. For her kindness, mother deserves kindness in return. For tenderness, she should be given tenderness. For her self-sacrifice, a little self-denial on the part of the children is in order. For love, she should receive an abundance of love.

Unfortunately, we often fail to recognize the contributions of our mothers until we grow older or until they are gone. All too often, we take these devoted women for granted.

This is one purpose of Mother's Day. It's an occasion for us to recall memories of mothers who are gone, to send loving messages to those too far away to visit, and to make happier and more cheerful the lives of those mothers who are near.

----

1. Proverbs 22:6.

A Glorious Name

I know a name, a glorious name,
Dearer than any other.
Listen, I'll whisper the name to you:
It is the name of mother.[1]

THE WORDS OF A CHILDREN'S SONG echo the familiar saying "There is no mother like my mother." And therein lies the sweetness of this glorious name. Children everywhere look to their mothers as teachers, comforters, counselors, and life-givers. They consider their moms to be "the best"—"the best in the whole world." And, for each child, his or her mom *is* the best. For where would we be without our dear mothers?

An old Jewish proverb explains, "Because God could not be everywhere, He gave us mothers." And, even while mothers cannot be in all places, memories of them and of their teachings can guide our thoughts and actions. Memories of mothers may inspire us to live more courageously, more righteously, more selflessly.

For most of us, our mother has been a steady source of strength: the hand that wiped our tears, the smile that lifted our spirits, the arms that held us tightly. She has fed our bodies, minds, and souls. Her words of encouragement and belief, her gestures of unconditional love and support were the first—and may be the most lasting. She has given her best; she has given of herself; and for each of her children, she is God's chosen vessel.

This message was delivered by James May.

In the final hours of Christ's life, while hanging on the cross, His concern turned to His saintly mother. Prior to completing His atoning sacrifice, He looked with compassion upon His weeping mother and lovingly entrusted her to the care of His disciple John. "Woman," He said, "behold thy son!"[2] And to John, "Behold thy mother!"[3]

It should come as no surprise that the greatest and most meaningful sacrifice would include the expression of love between son and mother, the remembrance of a mother's life and of her lifelong devotion. For me—and for every mother's son and daughter—there is "a name, a glorious name, dearer than any other. Listen, I'll whisper that name to you. It is the name of mother."

1. Frances K. Taylor, "The Dearest Names," *Children's Songbook* (Salt Lake City: The Church of Jesus Christ of Latter-day Saints, 1989), no. 208.
2. John 19:26.
3. John 19:27.

Mommy, I Love You

THE INFLUENCE OF THE HOME is a powerful force in our world; and, gratefully, its influence is generally for good. That good is tangible indeed; and, while the efforts of caring parents may go unheralded at times, without them the world would be so much worse.

Of course, parenting ideally is a partnership; yet who can deny the unique bond of mother and child. As one man wrote, "Mothers exert an influence in the world which is felt wherever human life exists."[1]

Such a pervasive, boundless influence ought to bring to mind, immediately and often, abiding and unfailing appreciation for our mothers—for their lives and the life they have given us, for the love they have shown, and for the countless other ways in which they have shaped us.

Oddly enough, we sometimes fail to see the great gift that is the culmination of daily acts of kindness, of lessons taught quietly in our homes, of sacrifices so seemingly insignificant that they sometimes go unnoticed.

Said David O. McKay, "Children accept [their] mother's . . . attention, care, and devotion as they accept the pure air and the glorious sunshine—just as a matter of course, as something which is their due."[2]

Sadly, if we don't take time to recognize all that our mothers have done for us—if we forget their gifts in the same way that we sometimes take for granted the very air we breathe—we may also forget to share our love and gratitude except when some occasion calls for an obligatory expression.

Every mother knows the joy of hearing a child spontaneously declare, "Mommy, I love you." Such declarations ought not become less common with age; indeed, they ought to increase as we reflect, with the perspective that comes from living a little longer, on what it means to have life—to have been given a gift so great.

We should never leave such expressions to chance, and we certainly should never assume that our mothers know that which we fail to articulate.

Whether separated by miles or some other situation, we should frequently close the gap and let our mothers know often of our love—both through our words and through what we are making of the lives they have given us.

1. Hugh B. Brown, *Eternal Quest,* edited by Charles Manley Brown (Salt Lake City: Bookcraft, 1956), p. 397.
2. *Gospel Ideals: Selections from the Discourses of David O. McKay* (Salt Lake City: Improvement Era, 1953), p. 454.

Remembering Father

A PICTURE OF HIM rests upon the mantel, hangs on the wall, or is tucked away in a photo album. For some, that picture may be found only in the mind and inscribed in the heart as a memory— or a wish. But, for most of us, the thought of our father can bring a smile, a moment of reverence, a tear of gladness.

We think of him whether he is alive or he has passed on: he who knows truth and lives it; he who has faith and exercises it; he—like us—who struggles to do his best and yet is not perfect. He's our dad. And we honor him.

To the father who teaches by example, who learns and loves, listens and cares, we say, "Thank you." But how can one day a year, one message, capture the powerful influence of a father? A lifetime of teachings, a life's measure of love, cannot be described on a page or returned with one grateful expression. His demonstration of integrity and service inspires us to be more honest, humble, and prayerful. His loving devotion to his wife, children, and so many others helps us to love. The greatest tribute to a worthy father is holding his name in honorable remembrance from generation to generation by living a righteous life. All that is good and noble can be the best inheritance of the best of fathers. Such is the influence, the eternal giving, of a devoted father.

For those who long to have such a parent, look to your Heavenly Father for wisdom and love. Go on bended knee to the Father of fathers. He hears your prayers, knows of your longings, and would have you honor your father "that thy days may be long upon the land."[1] Of all the commandments the Lord could have given among His sacred ten, He includes the honoring of our parents, the respecting of our fathers and mothers.

If your father has died, remember him. Talk often of his goodness. Honor his memory by living a life of great usefulness to the Lord and to your families. If your father still lives, enjoy your moments together. Cherish his companionship and learn from his experience. More than hanging a picture on a wall or placing a photo in an album, take hold of his life and love. Build on his service and sacrifice.

1. Exodus 20:12.

The Experience of Fatherhood

In THIS SCHOOL OF LIFE, we have a lot to learn. And so much of knowledge—of real understanding and wisdom—comes from personal experience. Mistakes made, lessons learned, and joys felt can never be fully understood or appreciated vicariously. Perhaps this is illustrated best in our roles as parents. No matter how many books we read, regardless of how keenly we observe, we learn the most about parenting by actually rearing a child. And that's the beauty of it. We learn by doing; we grow by struggling; we truly experience life by loving.

Today we talk more specifically of the experience of fatherhood, for the role of father is often underestimated. More than providing a living and meeting the physical needs of a family, a father's emotional investment in a child is vital. Many studies indicate that when the father spends time with a child from early on, not only is that child more academically successful, but he or she has more of a sense of humor, a longer attention span, and more eagerness for learning. Additional research shows that involved fathers help build a child's self-esteem, give the child a sense of his or her own value, and, as a result, increase the ability to resist peer pressure.[1]

Yes, it's one thing to provide opportunities for children; it's quite another to spend time—quality as well as quantity—with them. It's one thing to tell your children about values; it's another to live a moral life, where values define the way you live. It's one thing to tell your children you love them; it's another to show them love in day-to-day experience. In other words, the dedicated father who really shares his life with a child is much more to that child than just another "voice of experience."

One young man whose father died years ago cherishes the example of integrity, gentleness, and love his father left him. He remembers not so much what his father said but the way he lived, how generously he gave of his most precious assets: time, energy, truth, and love. These clear and poignant memories guide the adult son in his experience of fatherhood—and give him abiding feelings of gratitude.

As we pause to consider one of life's great teachers, that of experience, let us honor the fathers who are willing to share their lives and experience with a child. And as less-than-perfect fathers who learn and struggle, even while we try to guide our little ones, let us remember and look to God, our Father in Heaven.

1. T. Berry Brazelton, *Touchpoints: Your Child's Emotional and Behavioral Development* (Reading, Massachusetts: Addison-Wesley Publishing Co., 1992), p. 423.

Train Up a Child

PERHAPS THE MOST PRECIOUS MOMENT in the lives of parents comes when they gaze for the first time at their newborn child. It's a moment of joy that is filled with dreams and hopes and expectations. And it's a moment usually followed by panic, because being a parent is a job that doesn't come with an instruction manual.

King Solomon's wise counsel has given hope to parents through the ages: "Train up a child in the way he should go: and when he is old, he will not depart from it."[1]

Training children is the responsibility of parents. Each day, our children go to schools, preschools, and child care facilities where they learn many essential lessons. But these and other institutions will never replace the training a child can receive at home from loving parents. Marvin J. Ashton writes, "Home should be where life's greatest lessons are taught and learned. . . . There's no place on earth that can take the place of a home where love has been given and received."[2]

One way this love can be shown is by simply spending time with each other. Parents who share time with their children can have a significant impact in helping them overcome many of the problems they face. A recent study of junior high school students has shown "the prime determinant of drinking or drug use is how long the child is left alone during the week, and whether a child does homework correlates strongly with whether an adult is home to supervise."[3]

As parents listen, love, and train their children, it's important, too, that patience is shown. Our fast-paced world puts great importance on things that bring immediate rewards, but Solomon didn't promise that the fruits of parenting would be manifest after just a few days, a few weeks, or even a few years—but when the child was old.

Yes, the moment we first lay our eyes upon our child, we come face-to-face with the greatest responsibility we will ever know. And with this great responsibility may also come the greatest joy, because when we put our children first, we're building a relationship that will last.

1. Proverbs 22:6.
2. "Home Should Be the Place to Find Renewed Strength," *Church News,* October 10, 1992, p. 9.
3. "The American Family, 1992," *Fortune,* August 10, 1992, p. 46.

Safe at Home

WHAT IS A HOME?

"A roof to keep out the rain. Four walls to keep out the wind. Floors to keep out the cold. Yes, but home is more than that," wrote Ernestine Schuman-Heink. "It is the laugh of a baby, the song of a mother, the strength of a father. Warmth of loving hearts, light from happy eyes, kindness, loyalty, comradeship. Home is first school and first church for young ones, where they learn what is right, what is good, and what is kind. Where they go for comfort when they are hurt or sick. Where joy is shared and sorrow eased. Where fathers and mothers are respected and loved. Where children are wanted. . . . That is home."[1]

In the sport of baseball, the phrase "safe at home" is frequently heard. Indeed, that is the purpose of the game—to arrive safely at home base. That is also the anxious aim of weary business travelers everywhere and of tired children following a day of school or play. Home is, or should be, a harbor, whether its form is that of a three-story mansion or a three-room apartment.

And, while today's home and family may not resemble the traditional model—with father working outside the home and mother staying home to care for children—a home can nevertheless be a place of peace, privacy, and rejuvenation. The ideal home is one where God's influence is felt. Should we not, then, invite His Spirit to dwell within our residence? After all, He is our Father and is undoubtedly interested in helping us create a haven of happiness.

Grace Noll Crowell penned this appropriate thought:

> So long as there are homes where fires burn
> And there is bread;
> So long as there are homes where lamps are lit
> And prayers are said;
> Although people falter through the dark—
> And nations grope—
> With God himself back of these little homes—
> We have sure hope.[2]

With our Heavenly Father's help and by determination on our part, home can be a place where strife is shut out and love shut in. A place where friendship is found and hostility goes undiscovered. A place where self-esteem is built and insecurities are destroyed. True, it is seldom easy, but a good home never is an accident. Instead, it is an achievement shared by all who live therein. So, let us strive with patience, persistence, long-suffering, and gentle persuasion to create such an environment that we, too, will be "safe at home."

1. In Charles L. Wallis, ed., *The Treasure Chest* (New York: Harper & Row, 1965), p. 129.
2. "So Long as There Are Homes," ibid.

Spiritual Remodeling

PERHAPS NO MESSAGE is as timely, no truth more timeless, than the necessity of turning house into home. Yet, houses of learning, places of employment, halls of government, structures of society, and streets of neglect continue to act as inadequate substitutes for the most vital of all institutions: the home.

We may devote much of our time, talent, and means to the improvement of our dwelling places. We may concern ourselves with the condition of our yard, the car in our garage, the arrangements on our walls, the finishing of our basement. And rightly so. But do we tend to the most lasting, even the most essential, home improvements: the heart that needs mending, the self-esteem that needs building, the child and spouse who need our love?

David O. McKay explained: "Every home has both body and spirit. You may have a beautiful house with all the decorations that modern art can give or wealth bestow. You may have all the outward forms that will please the eye and yet not have a home. It is not home without love. It may be . . . a log hut, [or] a tent, . . . [but] if you have the right spirit within . . . you have the true life of the home."[1] A house may be well kept: windows washed, carpets cleaned, chimneys swept, and cupboards full; and yet, that very house may be in spiritual disrepair. While its body may be in good working order, its spirit may need significant remodeling.

Even while we consider the placement of tables and chairs, let us evaluate the real interior designs of our homes. Do the shelves store happy memories? Can ripples of laughter be heard through the doors? Does love shine through the windows and light the entryway? Are the walls thick enough to keep contention out—and harmony within? Do loyalty and fidelity decorate the halls? Is there place for quiet pondering and private prayer?

Such unseen accents are the beautiful building blocks, the crucial cornerstones, that transform houses into homes. For, as Victor Hugo observed,

> A house is built of logs and stone,
> Of tiles and posts and piers;
> A home is built of loving deeds
> That stand a thousand years.[2]

Peaceful and happy homes truly are indestructible, standing in the hearts of loved ones for generations to come. Spiritual home improvements, motivated by love for each other and for God, can transform houses into havens of security, shrines of joy, schools of cleanliness, refuges of virtue, and welcome abodes— even homes.

1. *Gospel Ideals: Selections from the Discourses of David O. McKay* (Salt Lake City: Improvement Era, 1953), pp. 480–81.
2. In Charles L. Wallis, ed., *The Treasure Chest* (New York: Harper & Row, 1965), p. 125.

A Checklist for Friendship

GOOD FRIENDS are a blessing. Their presence at life's wide table enhances all our experience, sharpening the joy we feel at happy moments while tempering our pain during times of sorrow. We may well agree with Aristotle when he said that "without friends no one would choose to live, though he had all other goods."[1]

Most of us would also agree with that great philosopher when he remarked, "We should behave to our friends as we would wish our friends to behave to us."[2] This observation is so fundamental, so obvious, that the expression of it almost seems trite. Naturally, it only makes sense to treat our friends with the consideration and affection we ourselves desire. And yet, it is surprising how often we neglect to follow Aristotle's basic advice.

A woman with a special talent for cultivating friendships recalls the uncomfortable surprise she felt when she realized that she, of all people, had slipped into a pattern of benign neglect where her many friends were concerned. She had become so busy with family and work responsibilities that she no longer did the things she used to do routinely: remember birthdays with a call, invite people over for an informal bowl of ice cream on Sunday evenings, pick a quick bouquet of flowers from her garden to send along with a note. None of these gestures was elaborate, yet each had been genuinely appreciated by her friends.

Ultimately, this woman decided to take the venerable Samuel Johnson's admonition to heart: "A man, sir, should keep his friendship in a constant repair."[3] She made a list of the qualities a good friend should have, then periodically checked herself against it in the quiet of the early morning hours before the noise of her day began.

Each of us may wish to develop our own checklist—formal or informal—with the intent of keeping, in the words of Johnson, "our friendship in constant repair." We can ask ourselves pertinent questions: Am I patient? Am I considerate? Am I courteous? Do I forgive? Do I really listen to the answers my friends give when I ask them questions? Can I compromise? Do I know when to say something—and when to remain quiet? Am I discreet? Do I know when it is in the best interest of my friends to mind my own business? Do I celebrate the qualities that make my friends uniquely themselves?

In the end, this kind of regular attention to friendship is nothing less than a standing invitation to the people we care about to join us and share life's many and varied adventures.

1. In Robert L. Fitzhenry, ed., *The Harper Book of Quotations,* 3rd ed. (New York: HarperCollins, 1993), p. 166.
2. In John Bartlett, *Bartlett's Familiar Quotations,* edited by Emily Morison Beck, 15th ed. (Boston: Little Brown and Company, 1980), p. 87.
3. Ibid., p. 354.

PART 7

Peace in Everyday Life

Life As It Is

AMERICAN ILLUSTRATOR Norman Rockwell is known throughout the world for his optimistic and affectionate portraits of life. His world on canvas depicts real people—friends, neighbors, and family—doing real things. During his eighty-four years, he painted more than three hundred covers for the *Saturday Evening Post*. And, while critics were often not kind, most people were instinctively drawn to his art. Somehow it reminded them of the goodness of life. As Rockwell once noted: "I paint life as I would like it to be."[1]

Yes, Rockwell could have easily painted, as some say, "life as it *is*." He could have concentrated on scenes of sorrow and moments of misery. He might have painted the mean and nasty, the cruel and depraved. His canvas could have been colored with conflict and despair. Certainly such hopeless hues could be found—both then and now. Painting his way through the Depression and two world wars, he did not live in a trouble-free world, to be sure! And yet, Rockwell chose to look for the good, the kind, the simple and happy moments that make life worth living.

Think what would happen if we chose to paint—in our mind's eye—life as we would like it to be. We might find more love, more friendship, more forgiveness—because we are looking for it. Perhaps we would appreciate more of the simple pleasures, small gestures, and gentle remarks that are directed our way.

Maybe the horizon would not seem so ominous, streets so dangerous, hearts so cold.

To those who argue that this "rose-colored" view of the world is not realistic, we acknowledge the ugly side of life. But beautiful things happen on ugly days, and joy can be discovered amid the sadness of life. Referring to Norman Rockwell, one art critic wrote: "He . . . reassured [people] of their own essential goodness. And that is a very powerful thing"[2]—so powerful that, for many of us, Rockwell's "life as he would like it to be" is somehow remembered as life as it really *was:* the "good old days" for which we may long.

But those good old days are never over. We, too, can paint life as we'd like it to be. And the more we look, the more goodness we will find; and the more "life as we would like it to be" will become life as it really *is.* And that's a very powerful thing.

1. "The People in the Pictures," *Life,* July 1993, p. 84.
2. Ibid.

Today Is the Day

So here hath been dawning
Another blue day:
Think, wilt thou let it
Slip useless away?[1]

THESE POETIC THOUGHTS from Thomas Carlyle tell of the promise of each new day. With every morning's light comes the priceless gift of dawn, the blessing of knowing that today is neither yesterday nor tomorrow. Today is now. And now is the time to live.

Yesterday, whether it was a day of triumph or a day of regret, is gone. We can learn from it and draw strength from it, but we can neither allow yesterday's rain to keep us indoors nor be guided by yesterday's sun. Basking in past accomplishments may keep us from striving for improvement today, just as consuming ourselves with past mistakes will make it more difficult to bear today's burdens—and to celebrate today's joys. Dwelling on the past may prevent us from believing in our ability to have happiness and to be worthy of God's blessings.

In the same way, when we live only for tomorrow, thinking "I'll be happy someday . . . when I finish school," "when I get married," "when my children grow up," or "when I retire," we forget the joy of the journey and lose the wonder of now. Tomorrow may come, and we can plan and prepare for it. But sometimes, with all the pain and hurt of this world, tomorrow may not come. So we must begin to live now—not in some distant future of "some-days."

Now can be the beginning of a new day, even a new life. But it is up to us to make it so. We can do with this day what we will. We can use it for growth and for good—or we can squander the present with preoccupations of the past and of the future.

Ralph Waldo Emerson understood this when he wrote: "One of the illusions of life is that the present hour is not the critical decisive hour. Write it on your heart that every day is the best day of the year. He only is right who owns the day, and no one owns the day who allows it to be invaded by worry, fret, and anxiety. Finish every day, and be done with it. You have done what you could."[2]

Yesterday is over; tomorrow is full of hope and promise. But today is the day to live, to learn, to love, and to rejoice.

> So here hath been dawning
> Another blue day:
> Think, wilt thou let it
> Slip useless away?

1. In Charles L. Wallis, ed., *The Treasure Chest,* (New York: Harper & Row, 1965), p. 221.
2. "Emerson, Essays and Lectures," *The Library of America* (New York: Literary Classics of the United States, 1983).

One More Day

Each of us has only twenty-four hours in a day. We can't buy or borrow more. Twenty-four hours is given to all alike. So, more important than the time we do or don't seem to have is how we use those precious hours.

We have all been torn by the demands of time. We all struggle to balance work and leisure, duties and desires, assignments and interests. At some point, we may be overwhelmed by the enormousness of tasks, the abundance of opportunities, and, through it all, the shortness of time. We may think of the talents we wish we had developed, the knowledge we might have acquired, work behind us and before us, and the good we might have done. With such a hectic pace of living, in the face of daily demands and details, we spend our twenty-four hours on some things essential and others not. The fact is, we are constantly—daily, even hourly—making decisions about how and where we will spend our time. To what will we give our most meaningful minutes? With whom will we share our sacred time?

This day, today, has been given to us as a gift. And, although time is limited and responsibilities are great, we can acknowledge this gift of twenty-four hours by using it wisely. Harold B. Lee encouraged us to "thank God for one more day! For what? For the opportunity to take care of some unfinished business. To repent; to right some wrongs; to influence for good some wayward child; to reach out to someone who cries for help—in short, to thank God for one more day to prepare to meet God." And he continued, "Don't try to live too many days ahead. Seek for strength to attend to the problems of today."[1]

Wherever our past may have taken us, and wherever our dreams may lead us, right now is the moment that counts. Today is the day that matters: twenty-four hours to use positively and productively—or twenty-four hours to squander and waste.

Most likely, our day will not be filled with astounding achievement and mighty miracles—at least not with events the world considers grand. But today's successes—though simple—may be grand nonetheless. What can be more glorious than a spontaneous act of service, a selfless word of encouragement, a heartfelt testimony of belief, a timely and timeless gift of self.

Yes, a generous God gives us twenty-four hours each day. Let us thank Him for one more day by honoring this stewardship—by making good use of our time.

1. *Improvement Era,* December 1970, p. 30.

Greeting the Day

Each morning, the American philosopher Henry David Thoreau used to lie in bed for a while and consider his blessings: health of body, alertness of mind, interesting work, a bright future, and trusted friends. After this moment of meditation, he would arise and greet the day, finding a world overflowing with good things, pleasant people, and promising opportunities.[1]

The way he started the day seemed to correspond with what kind of day he had. And the same is frequently true for us. Remembering what's right and good about life—first thing in the morning—will help us find goodness as the day progresses. We've all been told to "count our blessings" and "think positively," but have we considered the impact of beginning the morning with such a mental exercise?

Reflecting on what's right and contemplating the good requires real effort at first. Only practice will make it a habit. Sometimes it may even be difficult to recognize blessings. But, as we take time—each morning—to ponder our well-being, our minds will be invigorated and our hearts will be more glad. In Paul's words, we will "be renewed in the spirit of [our] minds."[2] The hopeful attitude with which we greet the day will, in large measure, sustain us throughout it.

Norman Vincent Peale describes the process well: "The more good news you tell yourself, the more such there is likely to be. . . . That which the mind receives upon awakening tends to influence and to a considerable degree determine what your day will be."[3]

Consider well how we begin our day. Do thoughts of happiness and success get us started? Or are we defeated before the day begins? The evening news and this morning's headlines tell us of all that is wrong with the world, but are we reminding ourselves of all that is right and good? Regardless of yesterday's defeats and tomorrow's challenges, we can find promise in today. Let us join with the psalmist and say, "This is the day which the Lord hath made; we will rejoice and be glad in it."[4]

1. Norman Vincent Peale, "Enthusiasm Makes the Difference," *Three Complete Books* (Engelwood, New Jersey: Prentice-Hall, 1967), p. 453.
2. Ephesians 4:23.
3. Peale, *Three Complete Books*, p. 453.
4. Psalm 118:24.

Worth Living For

We LIVE IN A TIME when we are choked with lists of things to do. Every day has its tasks—often so many that our best reward is just to cross them off our list. We add phones to our cars to get more done, learn how to prepare our food in a hurry, and eat in a rush. We want everything to be convenient so it can be fast. After all, if we run fast enough, we can get more done. We can achieve great things, build our resume, and feel proud of ourselves at the end of the day for a job well done.

Still, having speed in life should not be confused with having direction. If you don't know where you are going, any road will take you there. You can run very fast and end up someplace you don't want to be. You can climb a ladder only to find it's leaning against the wrong wall.

That's why it is vital that we pull away from the routine, take a deep breath of new air, and ask ourselves the question "What is worth living for? Since my time is my most precious thing, what is worth exchanging it for? At the end of this week, this month, or this year, what memory will stand out like a diamond in the sand? What will I have been glad I did with my life?"

Those of us who answer these questions often come up with this answer: It is not things that matter, it is not how much we get done, it is not the tasks we focus on and achieve that make life rich. It is the quality of our relationships—with each other and with God.

One man had a garden and yard whose care consumed his

life. Not a weed was ever allowed to grow on his grass. No branch ever grew beyond its careful trim. He could be seen out in his yard working almost any hour of the day. His high standards were commendable, but he never shared a flower, a vegetable, or his know-how with a neighbor. He couldn't be bothered. When he was invited to neighborhood parties or barbecues, he made it known that he didn't care for people and he wouldn't go. When a little girl's puppy strayed into his yard, he threw rocks at it, worried that it would destroy some precious corner of his lot.

Though his flowers blossomed beautifully, he became gradually withered up with irritations. Nobody noticed when he died, and his beautiful lot soon went to weeds.

Your relationships are not something to work into your life when everything else is done. They are the very center of it.

The moment we stopped to talk to a child, the unexpected visit we paid to a grandmother, the dropping by a neighbor's house on a Saturday afternoon—these are the things we remember. The laughing together while we did the dishes—even if it made the job longer, the day the family left their work behind to go fly kites, the nights Mom put aside evening duties to read bedtime stories, and the times Dad knelt with a child in prayer—these are the things we remember.

We have an expression that says "we should put first things first." Maybe it is that attitude, which has become so deeply a part of our world, that leaves us feeling uneasy and unfulfilled because it is not things we need to put first. Things decay, rust, and vanish away. It's relationships that need our highest attention.

Stepping Aside
from the Rat Race

··

It's a scenario most of us are personally acquainted with each day—the annoying sound of an alarm clock that seems to wake us too early to face a day with too many things to do in too little time. This seemingly endless, day in and day out routine has been christened by society, and it's known as "the rat race." Some have described this "rat race" as spending money we don't have to buy things we don't need to impress people we don't know.

Many claim to be innocent victims of this rat race, likening it to being a passenger on a runaway train. But that is not the case.

Numerous opportunities exist daily for each of us to step aside from the rat race. These opportunities may take only a moment of time, but they are capable of increasing our understanding of life's purpose and bringing us greater joy.

Step aside for a moment to notice and appreciate the beauty of the earth. Ralph Waldo Emerson understood this when he wrote: "Never lose an opportunity for seeing anything that is beautiful; for beauty is God's handwriting—a wayside sacrament. Welcome it in every fair face, in every fair sky, in every fair flower, and thank God for it as a cup of blessing."[1]

It only takes a moment to step aside and lift our thoughts to a higher plane. As the Apostle Paul counseled, "Whatsoever things are true, . . . honest, . . . just, . . . pure, . . . lovely, . . . [or] of good report; if there be any virtue, and if there be any praise, think on these things."[2]

And it only takes a moment to spread happiness to others through a kiss, a smile, a kind look, a warm greeting, or a heartfelt compliment; but the joy of that moment will long be remembered.

Yes, for many of us, tomorrow morning will begin with the annoying sound of an alarm clock that will come much too early. But, amid the hectic pace of the day, take a moment to step aside from the rat race. Enjoy the beauty of the earth. Lift your thoughts. Feel the benefit that comes when helping others. And then, in a quiet moment, take time to thank Him who has blessed each of us with all that is good.

1. In Ernest R. Miller, ed., *Harvest of Gold* (Norwalk, Conn.: C. R. Gibson, 1973), p. 11.
2. Philippians 4:8.

Ponder the Path of Thy Feet

An ADVENTURESOME HIKER prepared to climb a high mountain. He acquired all of the best equipment and trained for months, until he was in peak condition. Early one morning, he began the ascent. The first few days of climbing were exhilarating! He concentrated on his footwork, monitored his breathing, and enjoyed the scenery. It wasn't until he was near the top that a problem presented itself. He found himself at the edge of a cliff, looking down at a deep and dangerous chasm that separated him from the pinnacle he thought he had been climbing. With nowhere to go but back down the mountain, he had a day's worth of descending to do before he could resume the ascent.

What had gone wrong? Why such a detour? How did he get on the wrong path? were some of the questions passing through his mind—questions, perhaps, that each of us has asked. Like the hiker, sometimes we do not stop to evaluate where we are going until paralyzing cliffs of trouble and deep gullies of despair block our progress.

We may be so preoccupied by the pace, so concerned with our form, so interested in all of the equipment that we lose sight of the path. In the process of getting where we would like to go, our efforts—if not directed—may be futile at best and destructive at worst. We may be so busy going, so busy living, that we fail to design a life.

According to a recent survey, being "at the top" seems to have become less important to most of us. "The definition of success has changed dramatically . . . in the past five years—shifting from the traditional money-career-power orientation to one that stresses relationships, free time, and self-fulfillment."[1] More than ever before, we seem to be concerned not just about reaching personal and professional pinnacles of success but also about climbing the right mountains.

The Proverbs taught so many years ago, "Ponder the path of thy feet"[2]—stop going long enough to consider the direction our lives are taking. In careless pursuit, what appears to be the top of the hill may just be another plateau—or the wrong hill altogether. But with careful—even prayerful—pondering, we can find a path that will lead to real happiness and fulfillment.

1. "The Latest Consumer Trends," *Deseret News*, February 21, 1994, p. C2.
2. Proverbs 4:26.

The Habit of Enjoyment

ONE WOMAN remembers a simple, yet significant moment in her life.

As a student, she recalls living in cramped quarters on practically no money and spending a lot of time making plans for the future. Once she graduated, she dreamed of finding a job, purchasing a car, getting married, moving into a big house, starting a family, and buying a shaggy dog. Her dreams of a bright tomorrow helped her through the discomforts of a gray present.

Then, one day, while studying for an exam in her tiny apartment, a moment of significance came. Curled up in a tattered old afghan, she noticed how good the amber shafts of autumn sunlight coming through a nearby window made her feel.

"They warmed me from the top of my head to the soles of my feet," she recalls, "and I enjoyed the most incredible sense of well-being. It hit me then how many things there are about my life that I loved but that I often overlooked in my hurry to catch up with my exciting future."

A Chinese proverb has it that "people in the West are always getting ready to live."[1] Throughout the years, poets and philosophers have noted our very human tendency to overlook the value of the present in anticipation of the future. It is as though we sometimes put ourselves on hold until our lives are the way we want them—the way we've planned for them to be.

And yet, life goes on. It has been observed that "life is what happens to us while we are making other plans."[2] Indeed, the raw material of life is the present—the present hour, the present moment, the present second.

At times, we may find the present a difficult, even painful place to be. But taking note of the things we genuinely enjoy right now can help us cope. We can, in fact, cultivate that frame of mind which, in spite of our troubles, allows us to take a deliberate and thoughtful pleasure in something as beautifully ordinary as autumn sunlight streaming through the window.

1. In Robert I. Fitzhenry, ed., *The Harper Book of Quotations*, 3rd ed., (New York: HarperCollins, 1993), p. 262.
2. Thomas la Mance, ibid.

The Power of Routine

....

Routines can make life more predictable—and meaningful. Whether going on a daily walk, keeping a set dinner hour, or holding a weekly family night, routines bring regularity and security to our lives. When different and demanding schedules seem to pull us apart, well-established and purposeful rituals bring us back together.

The power of routines is evidenced all around us. One study of National Merit Scholarship finalists found that the only factor these high achievers had in common was that they ate dinner with their families each night.[1] Simplistic though this formula for success may sound, its implications are telling. Such families who consistently eat together do so as a means of exchanging ideas, sharing feelings, and acquiring support. If not, their shared dinner hour would be a meaningless and easily forgotten rut—not the purposeful and enriching routine it can prove to be.

A rut is different from a routine. Ruts are mindless practices, ineffective habits, procedures without purpose. And the regularity they breed can be destructive. Repetition for its own sake is not beneficial, but the repetition of significant routines gives our lives more reliable rhythm—something to come back to.

One couple who have been married well into their golden years live by such a creed. Each night before turning out the lights, they kiss and express their love for one another. With knowing smiles and twinkling eyes, they recount how this lifetime routine has strengthened their marriage—especially on those nights when they feel less than loving. Sometimes the kiss is not very heartfelt, and sometimes they even break into laughter, but the routine always seems to bring them back together. Their simple ritual communicates understanding, recommitment, and a willingness to start anew.

And so it is with all meaningful routines. Whether keeping a family dinner hour, going to church, reciting a favorite verse, or expressing our love, routines help us get through times of disorder and distress. As Sir William Osler explained, "Nothing will sustain you more potently, than the power to recognize in your humdrum routine . . . the true poetry of life."[2]

1. Catherine Johnson, *Lucky in Love* (New York: Penguin, 1992), p. 39.
2. In Richard L. Evans, *Richard Evans' Quote Book* (Salt Lake City: Publishers Press, 1971), p. 46.

Living Thanks

MORE THAN A FEELING of the heart, more than a vocal or written expression, gratitude implies action—literally demonstrating thanks by giving our learning, means, and opportunity away. Anne Morrow Lindbergh said it this way: "One can never pay in gratitude; one can only pay 'in kind' somewhere else in life."[1] Only as we give our grateful heart away—with kind gestures, listening ears, open hearts, even with righteous and prudent living—can we truly express gratitude. Instead of simply giving thanks, we must offer living thanks.

The Master Teacher explained it best in the parable of the talents. Before "travelling into a far country," a man called his servants together and "delivered unto them his goods." To one servant he gave five talents, to another two, and to another one talent. Upon the master's return, the servant with five talents had invested his gift and now had ten. Likewise, the servant with two now had four. And to each of these the master said, "Well done, thou good and faithful servant." But the other servant had buried his talent, fearing he would lose it. Ironically, he is the only one who did. The master took back the talent he had given him and, with it, rewarded the servant who doubled his original five. This more industrious servant had demonstrated gratitude by using well the gift that was given him.[2]

In the same way, when we are thankful for the treasures of time, talents, and means that bless our lives, we exhibit gratitude not by burying these treasures in our hearts—for our enjoyment alone—but by sharing them with others.

Anyone who has truly given or gratefully received knows that the most meaningful thanks we can offer is to use, apply, and develop our gifts. Children who appreciate their parents thank them by being good parents themselves. Spouses who value their marriage express gratitude by being thoughtful and considerate to their partners. Students who feel indebted to teachers apply precepts they've been taught to enhance their own and other's lives. Employees who are grateful for work say thanks not simply by completing assignments but also by giving each task their best. And so it goes.

Whether as parent, spouse, student, or employee, we convey gratitude not only by expressing but, more important, by demonstrating our thanks: by using gifts to give again, doubling rewards by investing them in others. For gratitude is more than just giving thanks—it is living thanks.

1. *Ideals*, November 1990, p. 19.
2. Matthew 25:14–30.

PART 8

Peace in Simplicity

The Simple Things

THE SIMPLE THINGS of life can be the most meaningful—even while they are sometimes the most elusive: a child's kiss, a warm cookie, a love note, and even a clean house. The simple pleasures satisfy our souls and may remind us of a less complicated time in life.

G. K. Chesterton wrote of our longing for simplicity: "The only kind of simplicity worth preserving is the simplicity of the heart, the simplicity which accepts and enjoys."[1] That is the kind of simplicity that endures. The deep and most sensitive places in our hearts are essentially loving and naturally giving. But sometimes those simple desires are covered with layers of sophistication and pride, scarred by sorrow and fear.

We all know that today's world is anything but simple. Just getting to work can be a complicated task: the traffic, the weather, the parking. Getting through the day may be difficult; the phone rings, the bus is late, a lunch is forgotten, and a mistake is made. With the high-powered pace of technology and the unrelenting flow of information, life may be less than happy.

We would do well to remember Thoreau's advice: "Our life is frittered away by detail. An honest man has hardly need to count more than his ten fingers. . . . Simplicity, simplicity, simplicity! . . . Let your affairs be as two or three, and not a hundred or a thousand; instead of a million count half a dozen."[2]

Even in a complex world, we can fill our lives with the simple things. By realizing that *simple* does not always mean *easy*, we can get back to the basics of good and of godly living. Instead of getting stuck in complicated routines, remember the larger and more meaningful projects for which you labor. Rather than losing yourself to your comings and goings, find happiness in the simple pleasures along the way. Enjoy family, cultivate friendships, and live right.

When we think about life from the Lord's perspective, it is really quite simple. Righteous living can be summarized in the first great, even "simple" commandments: "Love the Lord thy God with all thy heart, and with all thy soul, and with all thy mind. . . . And . . . love thy neighbor as thyself."[3]

Therein lies the "good news" of the gospel. Life is more meaningful when we lead out with love and truly follow our essential longings for simplicity—for right and for righteous living.

1. "On Sandals and Simplicity," *The Oxford Book of Essays,* edited by John Gross (New York: Oxford University Press, 1991), p. 377.

2. Henry David Thoreau, *Walden and Civil Disobedience,* edited by John Seelye (New York: Penguin Books, 1983), p. 135.

3. Matthew 22:37–39.

Looking for the Extraordinary

Danny and Reuven lived within five blocks of each other for fifteen years, but neither knows of the other's existence—until one day their baseball teams play against each other. And Danny hits a high-speed ball right into Reuven's eye. From such an inauspicious beginning emerges one of literature's great friendships. In Chaim Potok's unforgettable novel *The Chosen,* Danny and Reuven come to know one another as soul mates, and their lives are forever changed.

Reuven reflects on how "it all started with a silly baseball game." His father responds with a thought-provoking truth: "Reuven," he says, "as you grow older you will discover that the most important things that will happen to you will often come as a result of . . . 'ordinary things.' . . . That is the way the world is."[1]

All too often, however, we look for extraordinary events, relationships, and answers only in dramatic circumstances. We may discount the possibilities lodged within the ordinary or the commonplace. In conversation, we might deprive ourselves of life-changing insights if we listen only when something new and exciting is being said. In research, we may pass over an important "missing link" if a solution seems too simple. In relationships, we may fail to appreciate those who are closest to us while looking for more exotic and unusual connections.

But, thankfully, sometimes we happen upon a simple splendor that leads us to look for the extraordinary in the ordinary. For Reuven, it was a baseball game. For many couples who fall happily in love, it is an unsuspecting moment—an ordinary sort of encounter—that brings them together. For many scientists, it is a natural occurrence, such as a falling apple, a bolt of lightning, or the flight of a kite, that leads to a meaningful breakthrough.

In many cases, the phenomenal of serendipity, or the faculty of making valuable discoveries not sought for, is at work. Often, our desires and efforts are richly rewarded while anxiously engaged in ordinary pursuits. The extraordinary comes to us in roundabout ways: as a by-product of our labors, as a companion to our willingness, as a backdrop to our vision. No matter who, regardless of why, when life's most extraordinary events take place, they usually wear the pedestrian apparel of the everyday.

1. *The Chosen* (New York: Fawcett Crest, 1967), p. 107.

Transforming Events

THE SCOTTISH NOVELIST and poet, Sir Walter Scott, became famous during the first part of the nineteenth century not only for his writings but also for his graciousness. He was the consummate gentleman, never unkind or inconsiderate. Little children were drawn to him and adults were always eager to be in his company. He treated everyone with such courtesy and respect that he was considered to be "one of the great noble men of his generation."[1]

On more than one occasion, Sir Walter Scott was asked where he had been taught to be so kind. Instead of attributing a special academy or a private tutor, he recounted a simple but transforming event that took place during his youth. As a thirteen-year-old, he had thrown a large stone at a dog about fifty feet away. Aiming for the dog—but never supposing that he would make his target—Walter hit the dog and broke its leg. Even so, the wounded dog crawled over to him and licked his boots. The dog's kindhearted response to the damaging blow changed the young Walter Scott in a significant way. From that day forward, he explained: "I have tried . . . to have the same deep abiding love for every soul."[2]

Could it be that a simple encounter with a forgiving dog could shape his life in such a dramatic way? For Sir Walter Scott—and for many of us—the most powerful, even transforming events are usually couched in rather common circumstances. Life presents a series of meaningful moments that hour by hour, day by day, can change us. The friendly lick of a dog is just one example of an ordinary encounter that became a transforming event. As we look for and find the underlying lessons in our day-to-day lives, we may never be quite the same.

The greatest opportunities to learn and grow from life may come as we remain open to the many simple but transforming events around us. As we recognize the meaning in such moments, our character will be powerfully and positively shaped. For even a limping dog with a loving heart can be a teacher of truth and a catalyst for change.

1. Vaughn J. Featherstone, *Charity Never Faileth* (Salt Lake City: Deseret Book Co., 1980), pp. 11–12.
2. Ibid., p. 12.

By Small Means

In a world where we celebrate the big events, we often forget that it is "by small means the Lord can bring about great things."[1] Our heads are turned by thunder, applause, bright lights, and loud, insistent voices; we get beckoned by tempters and distracted by noisemakers. But that is not the way the Lord operates. His miracles are often quiet and unnoticeable except by those who have eyes to see.

A mother rocking her child, singing the soft tune of a lullaby, shapes a character. A small act of service changes a life. From a tiny seed bursts forth a majestic maple. The water dripping from a leaf eventually finds its way to the ocean.

If fact, it may be that the most significant things of this life are quiet, nearly invisible. Elijah learned this. The scriptures tell us, "The Lord passed by, and a great and strong wind rent the mountains, and brake in pieces the rocks before the Lord; but the Lord was not in the wind: and after the wind an earthquake; but the Lord was not in the earthquake: and after the earthquake a fire; but the Lord was not in the fire: and after the fire a still small voice."[2]

Another people who heard the voice of the Lord also reported of its quiet nature: "They heard a voice as if it came out of heaven; and they cast their eyes round about, for they understood not the voice which they heard; and it was not a harsh voice, neither was it a loud voice; nevertheless, and notwithstanding it being a small voice it did pierce them that did hear to the center, insomuch that there was no part of their frame that it did not cause to quake; yea, it did pierce them to the very soul, and did cause their hearts to burn."[3]

It would seem, then, that to know the really important things, we must pull away from the turbulence of our lives and take time to listen. The Lord will not shout at us; He will not compel us to hear Him. He will invite, persuade, whisper. His acts will often not be mighty and dramatic. They may be small, obvious only to the quiet observer.

Let us not be fooled by the loud hurrahs for the world that seem to capture so much of our attention. Let us not put our trust in the arm of flesh. God is over all the earth, and all His words shall be fulfilled. Though His is a still, small voice, it is the voice we can trust. Though He sometimes works quietly, it is "by small means" that the Lord brings about great things. If we learn to have an eye for small things, we shall come to see His hand in all things.

1. 1 Nephi 16:29.
2. 1 Kings 19:11, 12.
3. 3 Nephi 11:3.

A Smile Is a Street Light

....

Wherever you travel, whatever language you speak, a smile is a universal symbol. We all understand it; we each know how to give it; and we all love to receive it. Visit any remote corner of the world, walk down any street, start a conversation, and a smile says: "I care," "I'm interested," and "I'm happy to know you."

Shining in the eyes of both young and old, rich and poor, a smile is a conversational street light that opens the flow of communication, hastens a meeting of minds, and builds new friendships.

A smile gets us further in life than we may think. A recent study concluded that a smile "can make the difference between . . . a new job or a rejection, a lavish or paltry tip. The big effect is that the person [smiling] is perceived as being more honest, more trustworthy, more sincere."[1]

Experience confirms what scientists have proven. Not only do we feel better when we smile, but we also communicate caring, interest, and encouragement to others. A smile brings cheer to the weary, comfort to the discouraged, and hope to the despondent. People are more likely to confide in a smiling listener, reach out to a smiling stranger, and help a smiling neighbor.

Why does smiling have such positive effects? Because we cannot genuinely smile and think negative thoughts at the same time. We cannot extend the corners of our mouth without extending at least a part of ourselves. Like a hand that is put forth for shaking, a mouth that is spread in sincere smiling is hard to refuse.

By nature, we return smiles to their senders. And, if we refuse a smile by frowning, we expend more energy and engage more muscles than if we just let the smile flow. As we both give and receive smiles, remember: "A smile costs nothing but gives much. It enriches those who receive, without making poorer those who give. It takes but a moment, but the memory of it sometimes lasts forever."[2]

Like a warm ray of sun, a smile gently touches everyone—in all languages, in all parts of the world.

1. "Flash a Smile, and Jury Might Smile with You," *Deseret News*, May 14, 1993, p. A3.

2. In Charles L. Wallis, ed., *The Treasure Chest*, (New York: Harper & Row, 1965), p. 119.

The Joy of Laughter

WHEN SITUATIONS become tense and life seems unbearable, humor can work wonders. Have you ever laughed and reminisced with a friend, been to a funny movie, or read a favorite joke book—and laughed and laughed, all the while feeling better? The joy of laughter—if only for a moment—can help relieve tension, ease pain, and soothe an aching heart. It's become a cliche, but it's never had more meaning than now: laughter is great medicine.

Humor's benefits are powerful and long lasting. According to Dr. William Fry, from Stanford University Medical School, laughter is a form of physical and mental exercise. After studying the effects of humor on health for twenty-five years, he explains: "When we laugh, muscles are activated. When we stop laughing, these muscles relax. Since muscle tension magnifies pain, many people with arthritis, rheumatism and other painful conditions benefit greatly from a healthy dose of laughter."[1] A good laugh improves circulation, clears the respiratory passages, fills the lungs with oxygen-rich air, and can counteract fear, anger, and stress. Some have called it "internal jogging."

But, even while laughter is so beneficial and makes us feel so good, we don't do it often enough. Perhaps our hectic lives have made us so serious, so covered with layers of education and sophistication, that we have lost the ability to look for humor and enjoy the lighter side of life. We may be so busy being busy that we do not take time to laugh—even to smile—at anything, including ourselves. Of course, life has its challenges and difficulties, its pain and sorrow; but it also has its joy, its moments to smile and be glad.

Think of children with their ready smiles and contagious laughter. Even in the darkest moments, their cheerfulness is not far below the surface. They see the funny things all around them: the playfulness of a puppy, the tender teasing of an adult, the humor in a cartoon. And, in those simple moments that inspire children's laughter, we see the joy that is each of ours to behold. For, while there is "a time to weep," there is also "a time to laugh."[2]

In the words of Chester Cathedral's modest "Prayer,"

> Give me a sense of humor, Lord;
> Give me the grace to see a joke,
> To get some happiness from life,
> And pass it on to other folk.[3]

---

1. Terry L. Paulson, *Making Humor Work* (Los Altos, California, 1989), p. 66.
2. Ecclesiastes 3:4.
3. In Charles L. Wallis, ed., *The Treasure Chest* (New York: Harper and Row, 1965), p. 157.

Watching Our Words

L*ANGUAGE*," SAID NOAH WEBSTER, "is the *immediate gift of God.*"[1] That gift gives us the means to shape ideas, to share in relationships, to build cities, to make life liveable; yet, are we at times too careless in our speech?

F. L. Lucas stated, we "may take infinite pains about having style in [our] clothes, but many of us remain curiously indifferent about having it in our words. How many women would dream of polishing not only their nails but also their tongues? . . . And how many men think of improving their talk as well as their golf handicap?"[2]

So much could be said about speech, but consider briefly a few common concerns. At times, our speech is simply careless and flows too freely, which prompted George Eliot to observe: "Blessed is the man [or the woman] who, having nothing to say, abstains from giving us wordy evidence of the fact."[3]

On other occasions, our words become hurtful as we pass along to all who will listen what little we may or may not know to be true. Describing such tendencies, Alexander Pope said,

> And all who told it added something new,
> And all who heard it, made enlargements too,
> In ev'ry ear it spread, on ev'ry tongue it grew.[4]

Also, some advice given thousands of years ago still applies today: "Have you heard a rumor? Let it die within you. Never fear, it will not make you burst."[5]

We are at our worst, though, when our words become angry and then, too often, profane. The truth of the observation that "anger begins with folly, and ends with repentance"[6] should convince us to watch our words. We have often heard the advice that when emotions swell, when fists become clenched, we should, before we speak, count to ten, or to one hundred, or to whatever number it takes to soothe our anger.

As for the profane, the Lord stated unto Moses: "Neither shalt thou profane the name of thy God."[7]

Indeed, the Lord—whose words changed the world—set a standard for speech as He spoke with clarity, with firmness, with insight, and, above all, with love. All of our words ought to be patterned after His, particularly when He said: "Thou shalt love the Lord thy God with all thine heart"[8] and "thou shalt love thy neighbor as thyself."[9]

Were these two great commandments to govern our tongues, our words would always be a blessing—and never a curse.

1. *An American Dictionary of the English Language* (1828), introduction, s.v. "Origin of Language."

2. "What Is Style?" *Readings for Writers,* edited by Jo Ray McCuen and Anthony C. Winkler (Fort Worth: Harcourt Brace Jovanovich, 1992), p. 474.

3. In Emerson Roy West, comp., *Vital Quotations* (Salt Lake City: Bookcraft, 1968), p. 333.

4. "The Temple of Fame," *Pope: Poetical Works,* edited by Herbert Davis (London: Oxford, 1966), p. 70, lines 470–72.

5. Ecclesiasticus 19:10–11, John G. Snaith, ed., *Ecclesiasticus, or the Wisdom of Jesus Son of Sirach* (Cambridge: Cambridge University Press, 1974).

6. H. C. Bohn, in *A New Dictionary of Quotations on Historical Principles from Ancient and Modern Sources,* edited by H. L. Mencken (New York: Alfred A. Knopf, 1985), p. 44.

7. Leviticus 19:12.

8. Deuteronomy 6:5.

9. Leviticus 19:18.

The Miracle of Work

FEW THINGS satisfy the soul like an honest day's work. Whether we are cleaning the house, closing a sale, balancing the books, or plowing a field, great feelings of accomplishment and self-worth are the real compensation for labor. No amount of money, no sort of recognition can replace the sense of personal achievement that comes from completing a task. The assignments we accept may, at first, seem difficult—even overwhelming. But we all know how good it feels to look back at a finished project, realize what a difference has been made, and glory in work well done.

One extended family experienced the joy of work after spending a holiday cleaning. All of the children and grandchildren converged on grandmother's house for a designated day of labor. The garage was cleaned, windows washed, sinks scrubbed, and the house put into order. Adults retrieved forgotten heirlooms while going through closets. And children were told stories they'd never heard before. Working side by side, both young and old commented on how this had been one of the most enjoyable holidays they had ever spent. When leaving the home that night, everyone took a second look at all that was accomplished. They were exhausted from a hard day's work but exhilarated by the noticeable difference they had made. The soul satisfaction that came from hard work and selfless service left all feeling a little better about themselves and about each other.

Therein lies the miracle of work. The more we do, the more we want to do—and the more we are able to do. As we work, we learn, we enhance our abilities, and we become more aware of our capabilities. And, as we work with others, we can build bridges of understanding and trust. By extending ourselves physically, mentally, even spiritually, we feel gratified and realize the joy of using our faculties.

Ezra Taft Benson explained the miracle of work this way: "Energetic, purposeful work leads to vigorous health, praiseworthy achievement, a clear conscience, and refreshing sleep. Work has always been a boon to man [and woman]. May [we] have a wholesome respect for labor whether with head, heart, or hand. May [we] ever enjoy the satisfaction of honest toil."[1]

1. *The Teachings of Ezra Taft Benson* (Salt Lake City: Bookcraft, 1988), p. 481.

The Unspoken Word

In the early 1900s, the Russian pianist and composer Sergei Rachmaninoff wrote a series of fourteen songs based on poetry he loved. The final song, entitled "Vocalise," was dedicated to Mme. Nezhdanova, a coloratura soprano of the Imperial Grand Theater of Moscow. When Rachmaninoff delivered the song to her, she noticed there were no words for the music. Asking the composer where the text was, he explained that the message of the music was too personal for a text and told her to sing what she could feel. This she did, and the orchestrated melody is still played by symphony orchestras in many parts of the world today.

Words are often inadequate to express feelings and emotions that are personal. More eloquent than the finest oration is the touch of a hand for one who is discouraged or lonely; a smile radiating confidence for a frightened child entering school or leaving home for the first time; a quiet tear shed with one who has lost a loved one.

Music, too, can be more powerful than words, for it is an emotional language that can be interpreted however a listener may choose. It can carry a message of happiness and love, anger or frustration, or a feeling of reverence and hope in a sometimes dark world. Needing no translation, good music can build understanding among people and lay a foundation for peace between nations.

Could it be that the power of music comes from the possi-

This message was delivered by James May.

bility that music is discovered rather than created? Of his own compositions, Merrill Bradshaw, a well-known American composer, says, "I look for something that already exists . . . something I have known before that's waiting to be discovered."

May the music of this day fill your heart with joy as you reach out and receive the message that's there for you—perhaps a personal message just waiting to be discovered. Music is one of the Lord's gifts to the world that can bring peace to our souls. In Psalms we read, "O sing unto the Lord a new song; for he hath done marvellous things."[1]

1. Psalm 98:1.

Index

Index

Index